ETHICAL PRINCIPLES
In the Conduct of Research with Human Participants

American Psychological Association,
Committee for the Protection of
Human Participants in Research.

American Psychological Association

Washington, D.C. 20036

BF
200
.A46
1982
c.2

Copyright © 1973, 1982 by the American Psychological Association, Inc.,
1200 Seventeenth Street, N.W., Washington, D.C. 20036
Second Printing, 1984

These principles were adopted by the Council of Representatives of the
American Psychological Association in August 1982.

CONTENTS

APA Ethical Principle 9:
Research with Human Participants — 5

Part I.
Background and Methodology of the Development of the Ethical Principles — 9

Part II.
Introduction and Summary Statement — 15
  Ethical Dilemmas in Research with Human Participants — 16
  Elements of the Ethical Conflict — 17
  Two General Considerations Regarding Research with Human Beings — 18
  Balancing Considerations For and Against Research That Raises Ethical Issues — 19
  Correcting the Investigator's Bias — 20
  Individual Responsibility and Collegial Review — 20
  Responsibility for Assistants — 21
  Differing Research Contexts That Affect the Judgment of Relative Gains and Costs — 21
  Ethical Issues in the Sponsorship of Research — 22

Part III.
Explication of the Principles — 25
  The Decision For or Against Conducting a Given Research Investigation — 25
    Principle A — 26
    Principle B — 26
    Principle C — 27
  Fairness and Freedom from Exploitation in the Research Relationship — 30
    Principle D — 31
  Exceptions to the Obligation for Obtaining Informed Consent to Participate — 34
    Principle E — 35
  Ensuring Freedom from Coercion To Participate — 42
    Principle F — 42
  Protection from Discomfort, Harm, and Danger — 51
    Principle G — 53
  Responsibilities to Research Participants Following Completion of the Research (Principles H and I) — 62
  Clarifying the Nature of the Research to the Participant at the End of the Study — 62
    Principle H — 63
  Removing Undesirable Consequences of Participating in Research — 66
    Principle I — 66
  Anonymity of the Individual and the Confidentiality of Data — 68
    Principle J — 70

Index — 75

Research With Human Participants

The decision to undertake research rests upon a considered judgment by the individual psychologist about how best to contribute to psychological science and human welfare. Having made the decision to conduct research, the psychologist considers alternative directions in which research energies and resources might be invested. On the basis of this consideration, the psychologist carries out the investigation with respect and concern for the dignity and welfare of the people who participate and with cognizance of federal and state regulations and professional standards governing the conduct of research with human participants.

A. In planning a study, the investigator has the responsibility to make a careful evaluation of its ethical acceptability. To the extent that the weighing of scientific and human values suggests a compromise of any principle, the investigator incurs a correspondingly serious obligation to seek ethical advice and to observe stringent safeguards to protect the rights of human participants.

B. Considering whether a participant in a planned study will be a "subject at risk" or a "subject at minimal risk," according to recognized standards, is of primary ethical concern to the investigator.

C. The investigator always retains the responsibility for ensuring ethical practice in research. The investigator is also responsible for the ethical treatment of research participants by collaborators, assistants, students, and employees, all of whom, however, incur similar obligations.

D. Except in minimal-risk research, the investigator establishes a clear and fair agreement with research participants, prior to their participation, that clarifies the obligations and responsibilities of each. The investigator has the obligation to honor all promises and commitments included in that agreement. The investigator informs the participants of all aspects of the research that might reasonably be expected to influence willingness to participate and explains all other aspects of the research about which the participants inquire. Failure to make full disclosure prior to obtaining informed consent requires additional safeguards to protect the welfare and dignity of the research participants. Research with children or with participants who have impairments that would limit understanding and/or communication requires special safeguarding procedures.

E. Methodological requirements of a study may make the use of concealment or deception necessary. Before conducting such a study, the investigator has a special responsibility to (1) determine whether the use of such techniques is justified by the study's prospective scientific, educational, or applied value; (2) determine whether alternative procedures are available that do not use concealment or deception; and (3) ensure that the participants are provided with sufficient explanation as soon as possible.

F. The investigator respects the individual's freedom to decline to participate in or to withdraw from the research at any time. The obligation to protect this freedom requires careful thought and consideration when the investigator is in a position of authority or influence over the participant. Such positions of authority include, but are not limited to, situations in which research participation is required as part of employment or in which the participant is a student, client, or employee of the investigator.

G. The investigator protects the participant from physical and mental discomfort, harm, and danger that may arise from research procedures. If risks of such consequences exist, the investigator informs the participant of that fact. Research procedures likely to cause serious or lasting harm to a participant are not used unless the failure to use these procedures might expose the participant to risk of greater harm or unless the research has great potential benefit and fully informed and voluntary consent is obtained from each participant. The participant should be informed of procedures for contacting the investigator within a reasonable time period following participation should stress, potential harm, or related questions or concerns arise.

H. After the data are collected, the investigator provides the participant with information about the nature of the study and attempts to remove any misconceptions that may have arisen. Where scientific or humane values justify delaying or withholding this information, the investigator incurs a special responsibility to monitor the research and to ensure that there are no damaging consequences for the participant.

I. Where research procedures result in undesirable consequences for the individual participant, the investigator has the responsibility to detect and remove or correct these consequences, including long-term effects.

J. Information obtained about a research participant during the course of an investigation is confidential unless otherwise agreed upon in advance. When the possibility exists that others may obtain access to such information, this possibility, together with the plans for protecting confidentiality, is explained to the participant as part of the procedure for obtaining informed consent.

Part I

Background and Methodology of the Development of the Ethical Principles

All principles of the separate APA document *Ethical Principles of Psychologists* are subscribed to by APA members. Principle 9, the principle that deals explicitly with human participants in research, consists of ten subprinciples found on the preceding pages and hereafter simply referred to as principles. These principles are selected for more extensive development for several important reasons: These ten principles and their explication constitute the APA's entire position on the use of human participants in research—ethical guidelines, statements, or definitions from other organizations, institutions, or governmental agencies do not constitute approved elaboration or interpretation of this position; the large-scale involvement of psychologists in research; the researchers' professional consideration for participants; the pressures arising from public discussion of research; the enactment of legislation; and the adoption of federal guidelines for research with human participants. A workable set of guidelines that satisfies several criteria is therefore needed. The guidelines should reflect respect for human welfare and dignity, demonstrate awareness of the potential value of the products of research including dissemination of knowledge, and be relevant to all of psychology so that the problems of a few areas do not constrain the legitimate activities of others. The intended coverage of these guidelines should be limited to psychological research. The historical account now set forth outlines the events that have led to this document, which is expressly intended to satisfy the need for guidelines.

Recognition of the conditions that called for the development of the material in this document led to its beginning more than a decade ago. In 1966 the APA Board of Directors appointed an Ad Hoc Committee on Ethical Standards in Psychological Research, informally called the Cook Commission, which was composed of Stuart W. Cook (Chair), Leslie H. Hicks, Gregory A. Kimble, William T. McGuire, Phil H. Schoggen, and M. Brewster Smith. The method used by the Committee was patterned after that developed by the first APA ethics committee, chaired by Nicholas Hobbs (1952). This method had two distinctive characteristics: The first was that the members of the profession supplied ethical problems as raw materials for the formulation of ethical principles; the second was that proposed principles were discussed widely throughout the profession prior to their revision and final adoption. By following this method, APA became the first society to develop a code of ethics by means of empirical and participatory principles.

Two major advantages were gained by using the Hobbs Committee's method. First, beginning with ethical problems supplied by the members ensured that the principles would be directly relevant to the issues of research. Second, the participation of the membership in identifying ethical issues and, subsequently, in discussing and revising the proposed principles helped to increase sensitivity to ethical issues and consensus on good research practices.

In preparing the first published draft of the proposed principles [*APA Monitor,* 1971, *2*(7), 9-28], the Ad Hoc Committee carried out several operations. After reviewing the available literature on research ethics, the Committee designed a questionnaire for collecting descriptions of research involving ethical issues in the investigator's conduct toward the research participants. The Committee then revised the questionnaire after conducting a pilot survey of 1,000 members and sent the revised questionnaire to a sample of one third of the membership (about 9,000 solicitations). The resulting 2,000 descriptions of ethical problems met in research were grouped into categories for which the Committee attempted to draft appropriate principles.

The first effort to draft a set of principles revealed gaps and inadequacies in the supply of research descriptions. The Ad Hoc Committee's knowledge of literature on ethics and their extensive research experience suggested a need for more descriptions, for example, of research in community psychology, of survey research, of research with children, and of research on sensitivity training groups. Therefore, questionnaires were sent to a second sample of 9,000 APA members, and special requests were sent to selected groups (for example, the entire membership of the Division of Developmental Psychology). This second survey brought approximately 3,000 additional research descriptions, which, when combined with the initial 2,000, made an adequate corpus of raw material.

The Ad Hoc Committee also made use of the experience of scientists with a high level of exposure to a variety of research projects and with a history of concern for ethical issues: journal editors, staff members of research review panels, directors of large research organizations, writers on research ethics, and leaders in specialized research areas such as hypnosis. Ad Hoc Committee members interviewed 35 such informants.

Drafting and redrafting the ethical principles was a lengthy process. Distribution of the first draft initiated a process of review and criticism by APA members. Discussions were scheduled at many of the 1971 meetings of the regional psychological associations and at the 1971 APA Convention. State and city associations were asked to arrange for local discussions. APA divisions assigned committees to review the principles, and the Society of Experimental Social Psychology discussed the principles at length at its 1971 annual meeting. Psychology departments in colleges, universities, medical schools, research institutes, hospitals, clinics, and government agencies—800 in all—were sent letters requesting a group discussion of the proposed principles. From each such session the Committee solicited suggestions for revision.

The Ad Hoc Committee made sure that it would be exposed to the criticism of those with widely differing viewpoints. Individual psychologists actively interested in research ethics (for example, those who had published on this topic) were asked for suggestions. Also, members were asked, through the *APA Monitor,* to inform the Committee of problems that were not covered, of ways the principles fell short of useful guidance, and of means by which the principles might be changed. These requests for assistance from psychologists were paralleled by consultations with persons in other disciplines. Consultations took place, in some cases, through written reviews, and, in others, through face-to-face meetings with the Committee. Included in these consultations were anthropologists, economists, lawyers, philosophers, psychiatrists, and sociologists.

The response was extensive and constructive. Approximately 200 groups scheduled discussions and requested reprints to use for these discussions. A record of reactions and suggestions was received from 120 of these groups, supplemented by helpful letters from approximately 75 individual psychologists. The National Council of Chairmen of Graduate Departments of Psychology appointed a committee on research ethics (Rudolph W. Schulz, Chair; Martin Katahn; Gregory Kimble; Robert Sommer; Rains Wallace), and this group spent a day discussing the proposed principles with the drafting committee.

Working with the reactions from all these sources, the Committee prepared a new draft of proposed principles, published in the May 1972 issue of the *APA Monitor*.

Again the Committee actively sought the reactions of APA members. Letters soliciting suggestions went to approximately 800 psychological groups and to everyone who had made suggestions regarding the July 1971 draft. The *APA Monitor* carried a request for comments to all its readers.

Unlike the response to the 1971 draft, the response to the 1972 draft was light. Of the comments received, some indicated that reservations about the 1971 draft had been satisfied, some whose reservations were not satisfied indicated that the 1972 version was the best that could win general acceptance, and some indicated that the latest version permitted research behavior they considered unethical. On balancing the small number and the mixed nature of the responses received, the Committee decided not to undertake a major revision. Therefore, the 1972 version was recommended for adoption, as was a mandatory review at five-year intervals. With the acceptance of this recommendation, the Ad Hoc Committee was disbanded. The product of its work was distributed by APA under the title of *Ethical Principles in the Conduct of Research with Human Participants*.

The passing of the five-year interval and the increasing public discussion of the use of human participants in research led APA's Board of Scientific Affairs to establish a Committee for the Protection of Human Subjects in Psychological Research in 1978. The Committee was charged to make annual reviews and recommendations about the official APA position on the use of human participants in research. The Committee, therefore, reviewed and made recommendations concerning Principle 9, which is found at the beginning of this book, and then reviewed *Ethical Principles in the Conduct of Research with Human Participants*, which was the product of the original Ad Hoc Committee and which was found to need little revision. Most of the changes suggested by the Committee were editorial: keeping the code of ethics consistent with the explication published in this document. These changes were incorporated into the code of ethics that was adopted in 1981 by the Council of Representatives as *Ethical Principles of Psychologists*.

The review convinced the Committee that one major change was needed in the format of the document. That change was to forego the use of critical incidents to illustrate the ethics. In the 1972 version, the incidents were integrated with the text. In 1981, the Committee decided that a separate section on incidents would be preferable. Such a section could be easily brought up to date as new research emphases and problems develop, and it could comfortably employ incidents that relate to several points of ethics. The statement and explication of the ten points of research ethics entitled *Ethical Principles in the Conduct of Research with Human Participants* could stand alone as a booklet or be physically bound as a separate section with a collection of illustrative research incidents.

Several substantive changes in the explications of ethical points were made. The social context of psychological research, including immediacy of application, was taken more explicitly into account. Other sections were elaborated extensively, including those dealing with deception research, the sponsorship of research, informed consent, risk versus minimal risk, field research, and data bases. The Committee's influential input into the revised federal regulations on the protection of human participants in research has provided a framework for its revision of the present document as well.

The revision was submitted with all the changes to the Board of Scientific Affairs (BSA), the Council of Graduate Departments of Psychology (CoGDoP), and the members of the earlier Ad Hoc Committee. A notice of availability of the revision was published in the *APA Monitor,* and copies were sent to those who requested them. A first round of comments was received and the draft revised. To obtain a second round of comments, availability was again announced in the *APA Monitor,* and the revised draft was sent for review to BSA, CoGDoP undergraduate departments of psychology, state associations with ethics officers, all APA divisions (presidents and secretaries), APA boards and committees, presidents of other scientific organizations, and people who commented on the first draft. APA divisions were requested to announce the availability of the draft in their newsletters. Finally, an open discussion was held at the 1981 APA Convention.

The second round of comments was like that of the 1972 version—very light. Many responders indicated that the changes produced a better balance of opinions or satisfied reservations that had been expressed in the first round of comments. Therefore, no major changes seemed warranted.

The Committee for the Protection of Human Subjects, upon the approval of the Board of Scientific Affairs and the Board of Directors, recommended its 1982 version of *Ethical Principles in the Conduct of Research with Human Participants* for approval by the Council of Representatives of the American Psychological Association (August 1982):

Committee for the Protection of Human Subjects
Ina Bilodeau (1980–1982)
Robert F. Boldt (1978–1982, Chair 1980–1982)
Joseph V. Brady (1980–1981)
William R. Charlesworth (1980–1982)

Barry E. Collins (1978–1981)
Robert L. Helmreich (1981–1982)
Joseph D. Matarazzo (1978–1981)
Allan F. Mirsky (1978–1979)
Marlene Oscar–Berman (1979–1982)
Leonard Ross (1978–1980)
Sandra Scarr (1978–1980, Chair 1978–1980)

PART II

Introduction and Summary Statement

Ethical considerations always accompany scientific inquiry when it is applied to human research participants. Almost all psychological research with human beings entails conflict as to the relative weight to be given to one particular ethical consideration over others. For this reason, there are those who would call a halt to the whole endeavor or who would erect barriers that would exclude research on many central psychological questions. For psychologists, however, the decision not to do research is in itself a matter of ethical concern since one of their obligations is to use their research skills to extend knowledge for the sake of ultimate human betterment. Psychologists begin with the commitment that the distinctive contribution of scientists to human welfare is the development of knowledge and its intelligent application to appropriate problems. Their underlying ethical imperative, thus, is to conduct research as well as they know how. Since it is rarely possible to predict the uses to which scientific knowledge can be put, the scientist should not be asked to limit research to topics that appear to have immediate relevance to human and social problems. Nor should every research scientist be held responsible for making research applications. On one hand, in the social division of labor, some scientists appropriately engage solely in the advancement of knowledge. On the other hand, research having immediate applications frequently contributes to the advancement of knowledge as well.

Although scientists are obligated to advance knowledge, they should recognize the complex consequences of formulating what constitutes knowledge. Whether gathering information or sanctioning particular approaches to knowledge, scientists play a larger role as purveyors of scientific truth. Sometimes this truth conflicts with established nonscientific beliefs and values; at other times it supports and adds credibility to them.

Ethical dilemmas that arise in human psychological research should be faced directly and responsibly: Psychologists are rightly held to account for the ethical adequacy of their decisions in the light of the competing values and ethical considerations that are involved. The purpose of the present examination of ethical considerations and principles that arise in the course of planning and conducting psychological research with human beings is to promote explicit attention to ethical issues in their full complexity and thus to foster responsible decisions.

Ethical Dilemmas in Research with Human Participants

The scientific enterprise creates ethical dilemmas. Scientific knowledge and techniques that can be used for human betterment can be turned to manipulative and exploitative purposes as well. Just as the results of research in atomic physics can be used for the treatment of cancer as well as for destructive weapons, so methods discovered to reduce prejudice toward minority groups, to eliminate troublesome behavior problems, or to facilitate learning in school may also be used to manipulate political allegiance, to create artificial wants, or to reconcile the victims of social injustice to their fate. The double-edged potentiality of scientific knowledge poses ethical problems for all scientists. To the extent that psychological research deals with important problems and potent methods, psychologists must recognize and alert others to the fact that the potential for misuse of research increases its potential for constructive application.

The psychologist whose research involves human participants faces a special set of dilemmas. The obligation to advance the understanding of relevant aspects of human experience and behavior will, at times, impinge upon well-recognized human rights. Significant research is likely to deal with variables and methods that touch upon humanly important concerns. Psychological research often necessitates the manipulation of powerful and significant independent variables that make a difference in the world outside the laboratory. Answers to research questions may involve subjecting people to pain, to failure, or to stressful manipulations that could violate autonomy in the short run or could result in enduring change.

On the dependent variable side, research often involves the study of profound behavioral effects because the humanly important independent variables are ones that produce humanly important effects. Fear, embarrassment, aggression, blind conformity, cheating, and boredom, as well as the positive aspects of human experience and performance, become topics of study. The same considerations require the study of vulnerable groups—children and mentally disabled, poor, old, and handicapped persons. Some of the most serious ethical questions arise from the study of important problems in human contexts such as these.

Not only do ethical questions follow from the psychologist's pursuit of important independent and dependent variables, but the methods that are needed to make inferences as unambiguous as possible are often the ones that raise ethical difficulties. Many psychologists believe (although some question this belief) that to obtain valid and generalizable data, it is often essential that the research participants be less than fully informed about the study or parts of it. For example, the requirements of research may demand that the participants be unaware of the fact that they are being studied, of the quality of behavior being studied, or of the hypotheses under investigation. Even deception may appear to be necessary if a psychological reality is to be created under experimental conditions that permit valid inference.

Other ethical problems arise in connection with research methods: Experimental tasks or environments may sometimes be meaningless, boring, or otherwise unattractive to the research participant; some data that must be recorded and preserved for scientific purposes may later be used to the participants' disadvantage or for purposes to which the participants might object; the need to obtain observations on a random sample for the sake of statistical generalization may be in conflict with the ideal of voluntary and informed participation in the research; controlled comparisons may require withholding potentially beneficial treatment from some participants. This inventory of potential problems is expanded in the discussion of principles to follow.

Practices such as those just mentioned (failure to obtain informed consent, concealment and deception, exposure to stressful procedures and possible harm, invasion of privacy, withholding of potentially beneficial experiences from members of a control group) raise important ethical issues. Responsible psychologists will obviously invest their ingenuity in discovering ways of conducting research that avoid or minimize these problems. The ethical dilemma with which the research psychologist is confronted, however, includes not only the negative side—ways in which the dictates of good research come in conflict with particular ethical ideals—but also the positive obligation to advance knowledge of human behavior.

Elements of the Ethical Conflict

The ethical problems associated with psychological research on human beings cannot be solved solely by enunciating principles that point to rights and wrongs. When an ethical question arises, the situation is usually one of weighing the advantages and disadvantages of conducting the research as planned. On one hand, there is the contribution that the research may ultimately make to knowledge and human welfare; on the other, there is the cost to the research participant.

Within this broad framework of competing values are more specific conflicts, often between positive values that all would accept. For example, the obligation to obtain informed consent might require a researcher to tell participants that they had been selected for study because of their low self-esteem. To provide participants with this information, however, would conflict with the obligation to avoid treating them in ways that could be harmful or stressful. For another example, if an investigator learns in the course of a study that a participant has serious emotional problems, confidentiality requires that this knowledge not be revealed to others; but a general concern for the individual's well-being may call for communicating this information to the individual as well as to someone who could provide the necessary help.

In still other cases, the ethical desirability of using methods that would avoid misleading results may clash with ethical principles concerning desirable conduct toward research participants. One example of this type follows: According to the principle of informed consent, research participants should be allowed to refuse to participate in a particular study, to withdraw at any time, or to accomplish the same result by having their data destroyed. But the resulting sample would be biased in important ways. Especially difficult problems of this type arise in research where some treatment of potential benefit is used. Good experimental design may require that persons in a control group be deprived of the treatment for the duration of the study; concern for the deprived individuals may require otherwise.

Two General Considerations Regarding Research with Human Beings

These conflicts form the background for two general considerations regarding ethical standards for psychological research with human beings. First, given the initial ethical obligation of psychologists to conduct the best research of which they are capable, conflict is sometimes unavoidable. The general ethical question always is whether a negative effect upon the dignity and welfare of the participants is warranted by the importance of the research. Second, in weighing the pros and cons of conducting research that raises ethical questions, priority must be given to the research participant's welfare. The fundamental requirements are that the participants have made a fully informed and competent decision to participate and that they emerge from their research experience unharmed— or, at least, that the risks are minimal, understood by the participants, and accepted as reasonable. If possible, participants should enjoy some benefit. In general, after research participation, the participants' feelings about the experience should be such that the participants would willingly take part in further research.

Balancing Considerations For and Against Research That Raises Ethical Issues

Whether a proposed research project is ethically acceptable—taking into account the entire context of relevant considerations—is a matter on which the individual investigator is obliged to come to a considered judgment without abdicating this responsibility on the grounds of current practice, regulatory considerations, or judgment by others. In making this judgment, the investigator must take account of the potential benefits and possible costs likely to flow from the research, including those to the participants, that the research procedures entail.

As will be discussed in later sections, such an approach does not lend itself to any quantitative formula or decision rule. Further, there remain difficult questions as to how costs to the individual participant can be balanced against possible ultimate benefits to the participant, to science, and to society. A further question remains as to who has a right to make such decisions. Analysis of these questions also is useful in choosing between alternative ways of doing research.

Suppose that an investigator has concluded that the effective study of a particular problem requires deceiving the research participants. Among the possible costs or disadvantages of doing the research are that the deception might offend the participants or damage their self-esteem, lower the level of the participants' confidence in the quality of their relationships with others, or provide the participants with a bad example on which they might model their behavior. Furthermore, because of the deception, the research might give psychological investigation a bad name and work to the detriment of other researchers. Among the possible advantages are the potential theoretical and social gains from the research, the avoidance of misleading results that might be obtained if deception were not employed, and the research participants' opportunity to learn something about psychological research and to have the satisfaction of contributing to the social benefits provided by the research.

Such a listing obviously does not provide an adequate basis for the decision of whether a particular study should be conducted. The investigator must judge the likelihood and seriousness of the costs, the probability and importance of the gains, and the number of people who will be affected. Some factors can be assessed objectively and reliably. For example, the investigator can ensure that the individual receives whatever was promised as payment for participation. The investigator also knows the number of participants to be exposed to whatever discomforts or indignities the study may impose. Research participants and psychologists, however, may differ widely among themselves as to whether such experiences are perceived as harmful, inconsequential, or positive.

The same experience may be perceived by some as destructive and by others as a valuable opportunity for the development of self-understanding. Some psychologists argue that reactions produced by psychological research are so trivial compared to normal everyday experiences that research participants characteristically shrug them off as inconsequential. Although the theoretical and social gains from the research might conceivably extend to all of society, estimating the probability or magnitude of such gains or the number of people affected is difficult, and judgments will vary greatly from one psychologist to another.

Correcting the Investigator's Bias

Investigators should not rely solely upon their own judgments in balancing the pros and cons of conducting research that raises ethical questions. Personal involvement may lead to exaggerating the scientific merit of the proposed research and to underestimating the costs to the research participant. In addition, the investigators may be hindered from seeing costs from the participant's point of view because of differences in age, sex, economic and social background, intellectual orientation, and relationship to the project itself.

It is important to distinguish between costs as they appear to the investigator, as they would be consensually judged by colleagues, as they might be seen by members of the general public, and as they are seen by research participants. The gains anticipated from the research and the benefits to be received by the participants also should be appraised from each of these perspectives. The investigator also must recognize the possibility that both the benefits to the participants and the costs of their participation in the research may vary from individual to individual. When individual differences in reaction to research procedures can be consequential, the researcher is obligated to attempt to screen out of participation those for whom the risks would be high.

Individual Responsibility and Collegial Review

That investigators cannot rely on their own judgments to be unbiased underlies the recommendation that investigators turn to the advice of others. Psychologists and other scientists, clergy, lawyers, students, ombudspersons, and representatives of Institutional Review Boards are among those who might be used as advisors on the ethical acceptability of proposed research.

A recommendation to seek the advice of others on ethical issues should not obscure the point that whatever the legal or administrative requirements for collegial review may be, the investigator may not delegate or evade the responsibility for the critical ethical decision. The investigator should seek advice with respect to the potential costs of the research procedures to the participants, even if there is no legal requirement to do so. At the same time, the investigator should obtain as much information as possible about the probable reactions of participants. If the study is seen as potentially painful, anxiety-provoking, dehumanizing, or otherwise harmful, attempts should be made to adjust the research procedures. The investigator nevertheless must accept the final ethical responsibility for deciding whether or how to proceed. Collegial review can neither substitute for nor diffuse personal responsibility.

The type of consultation under discussion focuses on ethical issues relating to the research participants. It does not involve a review of the scientific questions of research design and analysis.

Responsibility for Assistants

The ethical responsibility of the investigator entails certain additional obligations to others. Research is often conducted by assistants and technical personnel. Such research arrangements impose on the investigator the additional ethical responsibility of making sure that these assistants conduct the research as the investigator would. This responsibility requires instructing assistants (and indeed all personnel) to be sensitive to ethical issues and, in addition, providing such personnel with appropriate monitoring and supervision.

Differing Research Contexts That Affect the Judgment of Relative Gains and Costs

The foregoing discussion has assumed the academic context typical of much basic research. The general expectation in such a context is that the research experience will not affect the participants other than giving them minor financial or educational benefits. The academic context, however, is not the only setting of psychological research. Other contexts include hospitals, mental health clinics, and other settings where significant benefits are frequently expected to be forthcoming; prisons, where ordinary freedoms can be manipulated; military, commercial, and industrial settings, where the employees have obligations to their employers; and cultural contexts where values, expectations, and language may differ considerably from those of the researcher. Furthermore, research (academic and otherwise) is conducted in contexts involving children and others who may lack full adult competence to evaluate the research in terms of their own interests. In all such contexts the participants may be exposed to risks not encountered in typical academic research with freely consenting, normal adults.

Research conducted in the context of human services (such as in that of hospitals) usually involves a mixture of potential costs and benefits that differs substantially from that of basic research in academic settings. For example, it may be important to test the therapeutic efficacy of certain pain-producing techniques in ameliorating a debilitating illness. The use of these techniques with patients is problematic because the techniques may compound the negative effects of the illness. In such situations, the investigator may feel compelled to expose patients to the techniques because no other alternative is available. The patient, however, may be more liable to discount the possibility of the techniques' negative consequences in the hope of obtaining the benefit of improved health. In such situations, the investigator must be very careful not to exploit the patient's willingness to take risks. In service contexts, in general, special care should be taken not to exercise subtle coercion upon clients by giving the impression that continued services are contingent upon research participation. The investigator must make explicit which services, if any, are by necessity contingent upon research participation, for example, if no treatment is possible other than the experimental one.

Research in settings such as prisons, military installations, and commercial or industrial settings, must be carried out with special sensitivity to the participant's obligations towards the rules of, or loyalty to, the organization. The investigator should also be on guard for the possibility of the organization's authority affecting the meaning of the participant's voluntary consent. The possibility of disciplinary action or loss of job security for saying or doing the "wrong" thing may substantially affect the participant's relationship with the investigator as well as the nature of his or her performance.

Cross-cultural research frequently shares the same problems as those in the settings just mentioned but may be complicated by the additional problems of the participant and investigator not sharing the same meaning and value of research or even the same language. Misunderstandings can easily arise in such situations. Participants may not give valid informed consent because they misconstrue the reason for and nature of the research. They may expect reward where there is none or may fail to realize before starting the full nature and consequences of the research operations. Negative long-term consequences for both parties can be avoided by the investigator's making an effort to understand the culture and being sensitive to its values.

Research with children, mentally disabled persons, and others incapable of giving adequate and informed consent poses special problems for the investigator. Special considerations and regulations appropriate for weighing the gains and costs of research in such contexts exist.

Ethical Issues in the Sponsorship of Research

The ethical principles advanced in this document for the guidance of psychological research have concentrated on the investigator's obligations to safeguard the dignity and well-being of the participants. Additional ethical concerns can arise in regard to the sponsorship of research. These include questions about the nature, mission, and administrative controls of the organization that provides financial support; concerns about the misuse of research results by the organization; possible restrictions on access to research data; and responsibility for promoting the utilization of research results.

If the sponsoring organization has selected the research topic, the research findings may contribute in one way or another to the mission of the organization. The investigator who accepts support from an organization should, therefore, be prepared to be associated with its mission as well as viewed as lending scientific legitimacy to its research efforts. Also, the organization probably will influence the research process itself through administrative controls in order to accomplish its mission. In such instances, the investigator should ensure that the scientific integrity of the research process is not compromised by such influences and that the research process, if so influenced, does not endanger the well-being of participants. The investigator should consider the possibility of these eventualities before applying to the organization for support.

The possibility also exists that an organization will apply the research results in a way detrimental to the participants or to society in general. Usually, it is difficult, if not impossible, to foresee how the results from a particular study will be used by an organization and what impact they will have on others. Knowledge of the mission of the sponsoring organization and of the impact of results from prior studies supported by it can help investigators anticipate the nature and range of the effects of their study.

Knowing an organization's policies concerning proprietary rights over research results before applying to it for support would also aid the investigator. Given that one of the fundamental purposes of scientific research is to advance knowledge and practice in general, the investigator should be informed of the granting organization's expectations concerning the immediate and open publication of research findings. Conflicts between the scientist's commitment to advance knowledge and the organization's commitment to its own mission can arise when research results are contrary to the interests of the organization. The investigator should explore with the organization the possibility of delayed publication or of censorship of results before undertaking the research.

The investigator may also be required to face the issue of promoting the use of research findings in order to benefit human welfare. Investigators differ widely in the strength of their concern for promoting such use. Some investigators feel strongly that their research findings, if beneficial to human welfare, should be applied immediately and widely; others conduct research without any explicit concern or plans for the manner in which their findings can be employed. In contrast to the latter, organizations usually have explicit concerns and plans for utilizing results, and these plans should be understood beforehand by the investigator.

Explication of the Principles

Ethical principles for research involving human participants are phrased in general terms. Hence questions will arise about their applicability to specific problems. The discussion that follows focuses on such questions and on factors that should be considered in answering them.

A section of the Explication is allocated to each Principle. Principles are identified after the section title in which they are discussed. Each section begins with a review of the problem or issue that gives rise to the need for a guiding Principle. Then, following a restatement of the Principle, a discussion relates the Principle to various problems, research settings, and populations of research participants.

The Decision For or Against Conducting a Given Research Investigation (Principles A, B, and C)

In deciding upon the conduct of a given research study, the investigator considers whether the planned design maximizes the yield of generalizable knowledge and minimizes the costs and potential risks to the human beings who participate in it.

There are a number of long-established and reasonably effective mechanisms for ensuring the soundness of the psychologist's judgment concerning the best ways to maximize the basic and applied scientific values of the research. Graduate training programs in psychology, critical reviews of research reports by editorial consultants for journals and books, and evaluations of research proposals by panels of experts who advise funding agencies all help investigators assess whether the results of an investigation will have scientific or practical value—though investigators should be aware that personal investment in their own research ideas may lead to an exaggeration of the potential contribution of the proposed study.

Scientific review groups generally are more concerned with scientific quality of the proposed research than with protecting the rights of research participants. Institutional Review Boards, departmental committees, and other groups for protecting human participants complement this concern by being dedicated primarily to safeguarding the welfare of human participants in research; but, the existence of these groups does not free the investigator from ascertaining whether conducting the planned research, including any pilot studies, would be ethically responsible. Are the risks and costs to the participants so serious as to rule out the study or to require an alternative design, no matter how great the study's potential value? If the research is done, might it harm the participant or contribute to a social climate of manipulation and suspicion? Is the psychologist ever justified in conducting—and perhaps even obligated to conduct—research that exposes human participants to severe physical or psychological harm? What are the possible gains from the research that its abandonment will forego, and what kinds of impositions on the participants or on society might be made by carrying it out?

When weighing the scientific and social gains from proposed research against the anticipated impositions on the research participants, some psychologists are inclined, at least on first consideration of the problem, to offer a simple absolute rule that one may never do research if it imposes some risk upon the participants. Further examination of the issue usually leads to the more complex judgment that there are matters of degree and circumstance that must be taken into consideration. Most human experiences and social interactions impose losses as well as gains upon the individuals involved, and research does not differ in this respect. Moreover, the decision not to act is itself an ethical choice that can be as reprehensible as deciding to act.

In drawing up ethical guidelines, one must look more closely into the specifics of each situation and its complexities. One has to take into account the nature and likelihood of loss and gain. Such accounting involves subjective judgments that are vulnerable to systematic biases. In order to reach a fair judgment in such cases, therefore, it is essential to employ certain procedural safeguards such as securing prior advice from knowledgeable consultants and obtaining the free and informed consent of the participant. Even using such safeguards, the investigator cannot abdicate final personal responsibility.

Principle A. ***In planning a study, the investigator has the responsibility to make a careful evaluation on its ethical acceptability. To the extent that the weighing of scientific and human values suggests a compromise of any principle, the investigator incurs a correspondingly serious obligation to seek ethical advice and to observe stringent safeguards to protect the rights of human participants.***

Principle B. ***Considering whether a participant in a planned study will be a "subject at risk" or a "subject at minimal risk,"*** *according to recognized standards, is of primary ethical concern to the investigator.*

Principle C. *The investigator always retains the responsibility for ensuring ethical practice in research. The investigator is also responsible for the ethical treatment of research participants by collaborators, assistants, students, and employees, all of whom, however, incur similar obligations.*

These principles assert the responsibility of the researcher for the welfare of the participants when the decision is made to continue, to modify, or to abandon the research. They also imply the need to consider specific circumstances and to take various safeguards in coming to a decision in each case.

The researcher's responsibility is retained through all phases of the research process and, subsequently, whenever the participant's welfare is affected. The further question of locus of responsibility for deciding whether to undertake, modify, or abandon the research arises when several investigators are involved in the conduct of the research (as coinvestigators, as senior investigator and assistant, or as teacher and student). Such collaborative situations multiply rather than divide the responsibility, so that each of the parties bears full responsibility. For example, both the principal investigator who designed the research and the assistant who conducts it are fully responsible for safeguarding the welfare of the participants. The following paragraphs direct attention to considerations that bear on the decision.

1. Types of Benefits and Risks That the Researcher Should Consider.

Conducting research implies various gains, including direct benefits from immediately applicable results to participants and indirect benefits from the advancement of basic knowledge. Furthermore, participants may benefit from financial payments or increased knowledge. Included also are the benefits to the investigator that come from doing the research. Conducting the research may entail a variety of costs: a reduced sense of personal responsibility, physical or psychological discomfort or harm, loss of trust in others, or invasion of privacy. Providing knowledge that might be misused or wasting social and human resources are also possible consequences of some concern.

2. Consulting with Others To Assess the Ethical Acceptability of the Research.

When to obtain advice. Although all research imposes some demands on participants, these demands are usually trivial and well understood by the person who agrees to participate—for example, when participating takes an hour or two and involves no more than answering some questions or performing a few simple tasks. No other risks, costs, or threats to the participant's immediate or long-term interests are involved. Even the most concerned observers probably agree that in most of the research reported in behavioral science journals, appreciable impositions are not made upon the research participants. As investigators turn with increasing frequency to research on questions that have immediate relevance for personal and social problems, however, the studies are more likely to involve procedures that raise ethical questions—covert observation, studies of ethnic and other group differences, intervention research, the use of concealment or deception, the invasion of privacy, the arrangement of stressful conditions, the administration of drugs, and other threats to the welfare and dignity of the participants. The investigator incurs a correspondingly greater obligation to consider alternative research approaches that impose smaller costs on the participant and to obtain the advice of others in evaluating the ethical acceptability of the planned research.

Reasons the advice of others is needed. The persons who propose a study may weight its potential benefits more heavily than would less partial judges for a variety of reasons; for example, the investigators' wish to contribute to a science of psychology, to alleviate social and human problems, to support their own self-esteem, and to advance their professional careers.

These same factors, plus any differences between the investigators and the participants in age, sex, economic, social and ethnic background, or intellectual orientation, may hinder the the investigators' accurate assessment of risks and costs from the participants' point of view. Research psychologists have an ethical obligation to recognize these potential influences upon their ethical judgments and to take steps to protect themselves from such influences by obtaining the advice of third parties who are concerned with the welfare of the participants as well as with research progress.

Advice concerning costs and risks to participants. Scientific colleagues will be helpful in assessing the potential costs or risks to the participants. Because they share many of the investigator's values and characteristics, as enumerated above, however, they tend to have some of the same biases, and these biases may lead them to minimize potential costs and risks to the participants. For this reason, whenever ethical issues are involved, the investigator should obtain additional consultation from persons other than scientific colleagues, who will adequately recognize and weigh impositions on the participants. The diversity of research contexts and the variety of potential costs and risks to the participants' welfare are usually so great that it would be inappropriate to specify any standard composition of a group of ethical advisors. Rather, the consultation that should be obtained in a given study depends upon the particular kind of cost or hazard involved in the research procedures and upon the participants to be employed. Professional colleagues with special expertise in personality and psychopathology, or about the participant population, may be helpful in assessing the consequences of the research participation. Medical consultation may be mandatory where certain types of physical stress are involved. Members of the participants' significant groups, for example, college students, minorities, or factory workers, might be consulted about possible effects on members of their group who are participating in the research.

The kind and amount of consultation and precautions required of the investigator are directly related to the extent of the potential costs and risks to the participants. Similarly, the greater the disagreement among various consultants concerning the extent of the costs or risks, the more carefully and extensively one should seek additional consultation and consider alternative procedures. Thus, while for most studies the investigator may feel that the costs are so inconsequential that no outside advice whatever is needed, research that involves a variety of risks and makes extensive demands upon the participants requires extensive consultation with persons representing a variety of perspectives. In extreme cases, where the scientific or practical value of the study seems very high but the potential risks or costs to the participants are also great, the investigator should not proceed without extensive consultation. In such cases, a continuing ad hoc advisory committee might be useful.

The voluntary and self-initiated consultation process that has just been discussed is quite independent of the mandatory review of an investigator's research proposal by an institutionally imposed review group such as an Institutional Review Board for the protection of human participants as required by the regulatory agencies or by the institution itself. An Institutional Review Board or the institution's own review committee may provide useful advice on ethical issues and matters such as the proper procedures for obtaining informed consent. The investigator may not, however, consider the approval of research by such a group as an ethical clearance that relieves the investigator of the responsibility for carrying out an independent assessment of the ethical issues involved. The operation of such groups falls outside the limits of a discussion of individual research ethics insofar as they are established primarily to fulfill the institution's moral and legal responsibility to human participants in research.

Ultimate responsibility. Regardless of the kind or the amount of ethical advice obtained from others, the ultimate ethical responsibility for the decision to conduct, to abandon, or to modify the proposed research falls on the investigator.

3. Responsibility for the Participants' Welfare in Collaborative Research.

Principle C states the ethical ideal for the not-infrequent situation in which an investigator is engaged in research in collaboration with another. Included here are cases involving coprincipal investigators, or a senior researcher and an associate, assistant, or employee, or a student and teacher in research assigned as part of an educational requirement. The principle states the demanding but unavoidable rule that responsibility can only be multiplied, never divided, by such collaboration. We examine below several aspects of ethical responsibility in collaborative research.

The principal investigator's responsibility. The senior investigator who designs the study but has the data collection carried out by collaborators, associates, students, or employees is as responsible for the humane treatment of the participants as if she or he collected the data. A principal investigator has the obligation to train assistants and students so that they will be ethically responsible and must supervise them sufficiently to ensure that the participants are being well treated. Graduate and undergraduate training in psychological research should be designed to ensure that the students are as able and motivated to do research ethically as they are to do it skillfully.

Assistant's responsibility. The fact that, in such collaborative research efforts, the principal investigator or teacher retains responsibility for the humane treatment of the participants does not relieve the assistant or student of equal responsibility. That is, the student or assistant should be as sensitive to, and solicitous of, the welfare of the participants as if the research project were solely the student's or assistant's own. To say that one was ordered to perform such actions by an employer or teacher in no way excuses one's impositions on research participants.

Supervisor's responsibility. The teacher or research supervisor should respect the moral judgment of students and assistants. If students or assistants feel a moral reluctance to carry out a research procedure, the supervisor should not pressure them to perform the procedure, even though it seems completely acceptable.

Fairness and Freedom from Exploitation in the Research Relationship (Principle D)

The relationship between the investigator and the research participant is one of mutual respect and involves considerations of fairness or equity. Each party to the relationship has expectations of the other, which in the ideal case will be accurate and congruent with one another. The agreement to take part in an experiment usually implies that participants are willing to give their time and perhaps to experience unpleasantness or risk. Participants may receive tangible rewards, personal help (such as counseling or therapy), information (such as an explanation of the purposes of the experiment and its relationship to the current state of knowledge in some field). Participants also may wish to help advance science or solve a social problem. Ethical problems arise when investigators violate the agreement or exploit the participants' personal circumstances in order to obtain cooperation.

The agreement between the investigator and the research participant can be evaluated from a dual perspective: (1) The agreement itself should be fair in the judgment of the participant; (2) the investigator should keep whatever promises are made. Although ideally there should be a reciprocal provision of benefits and good faith on the part of the participant, the concern here is only with the obligations of the investigator.

The researcher's obligations to the research participant are frequently not easy to establish with clarity for several reasons: (1) The expected and actual benefits to the participants are difficult to assess; (2) some potential participants—for example, children and mentally disabled persons—may not be able to understand the proposed agreement; (3) the personal situation of the individual may influence what seems fair (for example, a person feeling great need of some service such as psychotherapy would be willing to take greater risks and to sustain greater costs to obtain this help than would a person without such a felt need); and (4) finally, some of the investigator's obligations exist only because of the implications of the research setting (e.g., correctional institutions involve different obligations from those in employment contexts). Such intangibles are, of course, particularly difficult to assess.

How explicit does the agreement between investigator and participant need to be? How can the investigator tread the thin line between offering adequate inducements to participate and coercing or exploiting the participant (see Principle F)? When the possibility of exploitation is manifest, how may the responsible investigator nevertheless safeguard the interests of the participant?

Ethical investigators must be concerned with the fairness of whatever implicit or explicit agreements are made with the participants. They incur the responsibility of ensuring that the participants' reasonable expectations are realized. In appraising the fairness of the agreement, the investigator must guard against exploiting the special needs and vulnerabilities of the potential participants to gain their cooperation. The guiding principle can be stated thus:

Principle D. *Except in minimal-risk research, the investigator establishes a clear and fair agreement with research participants, prior to their participation, that clarifies the obligations and responsibilities of each. The investigator has the obligation to honor all promises and commitments included in that agreement. The investigator informs the participants of all aspects of the research that might reasonably be expected to influence willingness to participate and explains all other aspects of the research about which the participants inquire. Failure to make full disclosure prior to obtaining informed consent requires additional safeguards to protect the welfare and dignity of the research participants. Research with children or with participants who have impairments that would limit understanding and/or communication requires special safeguard procedures.*

Principle D states the three essential components of an appropriate agreement between investigator and participant: that the terms of the agreement be clear and explicit, that they be basically fair and not exploitive, and that the investigator honor the agreement.

1. The Explicitness of the Agreement.

Explicitness is only another way of looking at the problems of informed consent and freedom from coercion to participate, which are treated at length under Principles E and F. Sometimes there are reasons an investigator may responsibly decide that compromising these ideals with respect to either the information provided or the opportunity for free consent is warranted; however, when the possible costs to the participant are more than trivial, the investigator incurs serious ethical responsibility if the participant is deprived of these rights. By the same token, the more substantial the possible costs to the participants of their research involvement, the more essential it is that the research agreement be fully explicit. The kinds of procedures discussed under Principle F in connection with the administration of a "subject pool" for research on students in a university setting help ensure a desirable degree of explicitness.

2. The Relationship Between the Participants' Needs and the Benefits Received.

In many research situations, a congruent relationship exists between the needs of the participants and the type of benefits offered. But in other cases, the relationship is not congruent. For students in introductory psychology, for example, participation might provide a benefit relevant to the need that led them into the course in the first place—the desire for psychological knowledge. Rewarding such students directly in these terms seems appropriate. Whether or not the knowledge provided is exactly coincident with the specific subject matter of the course, working out an explanation of the investigation to contribute to the students' psychological education should be a straightforward matter and a felt obligation for the researcher. (See pages 47–48.)

Inducing participation in anticipation of benefits to the participants' major reference groups is in violation of Principle D unless the investigator is in a confident position to deliver on this promise.

Special problems arise when the researcher artificially creates needs (usually in the process of recruiting) that may then enter into the participants' perception of the agreement with the investigator, for example, suggesting that declining to participate is a sign of weakness or immaturity. Such tactics not only involve an inappropriately coercive threat, but they also imply that cooperation in the experiment will be rewarded by more favorable perception of the participants by their peers, by the investigator, or by the staff.

Governmental regulatory agencies and many institutions that have regulations for non-federally funded research require that informed consent statements contain an instruction that the participant is free to withdraw consent and to discontinue participation in the project or activity at any time without affecting the individual's status or legal rights. In addition, patients are told that withdrawal of participation will not jeopardize treatment in any way.

3. Fulfilling the Agreement with the Participant.

Clearly, an agreement between investigator and participant involves more than the promises directly related to the research procedures. Part of what is involved is covered in the previous section, where it is illustrated that taking advantage of strong needs to induce individuals to participate without their being adequately free to refuse may create expectations in the participant that the investigator cannot fulfill. Moreover, research takes place in a social context which has its own inherent implications. For example, participants rightfully anticipate respectful treatment. Because the investigator pays the participants or exacts required research participation from them, the possibility always exists that this payment or demand will be accepted by both parties as the entire definition of the relationship. The intent of Principle D, however, is broader than such definition.

4. Classes of Participants Whose Own Consent Must Be Supplemented by That of Another.

Legally, as well as ethically, some potential participants in psychological research do not have the competence to give their informed consent. The problem arises with children and legal minors, with mentally disabled persons, and with prisoners. Sound practice from a legal standpoint requires that the informed consent of the legal guardian or other authority be obtained for such an individual's research participation; the corresponding ethical consideration holds that free and informed consent should be obtained from a person whose primary interest is in the participant's welfare.

Even in the case of legally incompetent persons, consent on the part of a parent or guardian does not obviate the need to provide information understandable to the potential participant whose wishes are to be respected. If a child or a mentally disabled person is capable of making some reasonable judgment concerning the nature of the research and of participation in it, permission should be obtained from the participant as well as from the responsible adult or guardian. Colleagues or Institutional Review Boards may be helpful in clarifying instances of an ambiguous nature.

Exceptions to the Obligation for Obtaining Informed Consent to Participate (Including Issues of Concealment and Deception) (Principle E)

Many ethical issues are resolved if a scientific investigation rests on the researcher's fully informed and competent decision to investigate and the participants' fully informed and competent decision to be investigated. If participants are placed at more than minimal risk (Principle B), the investigator designs methods to inform participants of those risks (Principle D). As already discussed, Principle D details the obligation to inform prospective participants of all features of the research that reasonably might be expected to influence willingness to participate in the research. Principle F (discussed on pages 42–51) stresses the investigator's obligation to respect the individual's freedom to withdraw from the research at any time. Investigators are further obligated to assure themselves that prospective participants are of sufficient age and mental and emotional maturity that they are competent to make an informed decision to participate. As previously detailed, the decision to participate should reflect an informed judgment by individuals that participation will not compromise their own self-interest.

Ethical problems may arise, however, because the requirements of effective psychological research sometimes conflict with the simple fulfillment of the obligation to obtain informed consent. Principle E covers situations in which methodological requirements make fully informed consent impracticable. For example, the relevant information may be too technical for the person to evaluate, as in most tests of quantitative hypotheses when the theory may be beyond the research participant's comprehension. Psychophysiological studies may involve processes completely unfamiliar to the participant. In many cases, the degree of potential discomfort, harm, or embarrassment relevant to the decision to participate may not be fully ascertainable prior to the conduct of the research. Certain classes of people (e.g., children and mentally disabled persons) may be incapable of responsible decisions.

The most common reason for limiting information, however, is that valid data could not be obtained if the participant were fully informed about the purposes and procedures of the research and the experiences to be anticipated. Methodological requirements of the research may demand that the participants remain unaware of the fact that they are being studied or of the specific hypotheses under investigation. Incomplete information or misinformation may have to be provided to elicit the behavior of a naive individual or to create a psychological reality under conditions that permit valid inference.

These valid research requirements present the investigator with ethical dilemmas. Under what circumstances, if any, is it acceptable to bypass, delay, or compromise acting on the obligation to give participants full information about the research and to obtain the required consent or refusal to participate? About what aspects of the research must information be provided? The issues involved here are closely entwined with ones subsequently examined under Principle F, Ensuring Freedom from Coercion To Participate. They also touch upon considerations relating to the responsibility of the investigator to provide clarifying information at the end of a study (Principle H, pages 62–66). Since deception employed in research intrinsically compromises the agreement on which consent is based, and also can involve "bad faith" which raises a second and more serious ethical concern, a separate principle, Principle E, is devoted to deception.

Some would say that research is always ethical if it involves a researcher's fully informed and competent decision to conduct the research and a participant's fully informed and competent decision to participate—regardless of the stressful or aversive consequences to the participant. Many people believe that informed consent is a necessary but not sufficient condition and that other factors (for example, alternative procedures, or importance of data) must also be considered. Others would raise the principle of informed consent to the level where research can be conducted if, and only if, informed consent has been obtained. This latter view would eliminate all deception and concealment. Principle D details the desirability of informed consent. Principle E deals with situations in which informed consent is not easily obtained.

Clearly the ethical ideal of obtaining fully informed consent cannot be realized in some research without the possibility that the results of the research will be deceptive or misleading. In addition, technical aspects of the research may exceed the limits of what participants can comprehend.

Principle E. ***Methodological requirements of a study may make the use of concealment or deception necessary. Before conducting such a study, the investigator has a special responsibility to (1) determine whether the use of such techniques is*** *justified by the study's prospective scientific, educational, or applied value; (2) determine whether alternative procedures are available that do not use concealment or deception; and (3) ensure that the participants are provided with sufficient explanation as soon as possible.*

Providing complete information about all of the considerations that might be important to potential participants is obviously impracticable and unacceptable to the research participant and the investigator alike. It is often desirable, however, for the investigator to double-check his or her judgment in this respect by consulting with qualified others and by responding fully to the potential participants' questions about the research.

Some psychologists feel that respect for the dignity of the individual allows no compromise of the principle of informed consent. Others argue with equal conviction that society's interest in the advancement of scientific knowledge of human behavior often justifies some compromise of the ideal of providing complete information in advance—especially with minimal risk research. Principle D reminds the investigator of the responsiblity to inform the research participants of every aspect of the research that might affect willingness to participate, including the fact that some information must be withheld. If scientific considerations dictate the withholding of information, ethical responsibility requires the investigator to assume personal responsibility for a careful weighing of the scientific requirements of the situation against the ethical requirements of the situation and for a careful consideration of alternative research questions and methodologies that would allow informed consent. Investigators who cannot resolve the conflict about withholding information should seek the advice of others, including persons with different perspectives on values (Principle A).

    1. Involvement of Persons in Research without Their Knowledge or Consent.

In some research situations, participants may be unaware that they are being studied; Principle D, which relates to informed consent, must be regarded in some sense as not applicable in these cases.

The motivation to conceal from the person even the fact of participation in a research activity arises most frequently when the investigator feels such knowledge will influence behavior to such an extent that the research objectives cannot be reached. Studying some phenomena seems impossible if the individual is aware that a study is being made. This difficulty has led to concealment of research activity in several ways. Records of covert or participant observations, data from disguised field experiments or research manipulations added to existing nonresearch operations, and information from third parties can yield data in natural settings that would be unattainable or seriously confounded if the subjects were aware of the presence of an investigator.

Covert or unobtrusive observation or recording of public behavior. In order to obtain direct, firsthand information uninfluenced by awareness of the data-collection process, psychologists may wish to enter a natural situation under an assumed identity or, at least, without revealing their research interests. In other cases, the effort to obtain records of natural behavior uninfluenced by the recording process may lead investigators to use concealed recording procedures to document aspects of behavior of persons who are not informed about the recording process. Under what circumstances, if ever, is the investigator justified in adopting such procedures? The ethical problem is greatly alleviated when the data are collected in such a way that respondents cannot easily be connected with the data gathered on them. Under these conditions of anonymity and with otherwise minimal risks to the participant, many psychologists feel the concealment is ethically acceptable. The involvement of individuals in this sort of research is minimal and is not comparable to that of research participants in the usual sense. The experience of the participants is not affected by the research, and there are no direct positive or negative effects on them. Cases involving anonymous observation of public behavior approach that of historical research (in which the public acts of persons are studied without their consent being thought at all necessary) or that of research with unobtrusive measures, where inferences are drawn from the "traces that people leave" without anyone's actual participation in the research.

It should also be recognized that covert nonanonymous recording complicates the matter, because the record is potentially permanent and poses a long-term threat to the privacy of the persons observed. Such recording also adds to the problem of maintaining confidentiality (see pages 68–74). A request for permission to keep or use the records shows sensitivity to this issue. Linkage of observations with official files and direct questionnaire inquiry raises more serious questions. Observation with hidden cameras or microphones is personally objectionable to many people, whether the observation is for research purposes or not. When such individuals can be identified in film or tape records, such invasion of privacy could yield information that might be used against the observed individual. Whether such information is identifiable or not, common acceptance of such practices might adversely affect attitudes of trust in interpersonal relationships. In terms of this argument, covert observation paves the road to a society in which individuals are under constant surveillance. Whether or not this argument is valid is irrelevant; some people accept the argument, and Principle E implies that such a possibility must be taken into account in the ethical analysis preceding the use of covert observation.

Disguised field experimentation in public situations. This section concerns research in which the investigator not only records the behavior of unsuspecting individuals but also covertly arranges or manipulates their experiences. Encouragement from the broader society to make psychological research relevant to urgent social problems may foster this type of research.

When the "person in the street" becomes a participant in research, informed consent can be difficult to obtain. Sometimes, however, an innovative investigator can obtain informed consent. For example, teachers in a school might agree to be subjects in a naturalistic experiment without knowing the independent variable, the dependent variable, or the time and place in which research will take place. In the least questionable cases, neither the anonymity nor the personal integrity of the participant are violated, and patience is only trivially imposed upon. But offenses to human dignity and other risks to participants are readily imaginable in this sort of experimentation. If such procedures become more numerous in an effort to obtain information about important social issues, their cumulative effect may undermine confidence in human relationships. Because of these ethical complexities and because of possible biases on the part of investigators, such research may be considered only with misgivings, and then only when alternative methodologies or research problems have been carefully evaluated.

Covert or participant observation in private situations. In public situations, participants are at least aware that others will likely observe them—even if they are not aware that their behavior will be recorded and used for research purposes. In private situations, however, participants believe they have no audience, that is, their behavior is not observed. Ethical issues raised by covert or participant observation in private situations are therefore especially problematic, particularly when participants are allowed to make self-revelations they would not have made had informed consent been obtained. Even more difficult to justify ethically is research in private situations in which the investigator actively entices participants to behave in such a way as to make self-revelations that would not have been made without intervention by the investigator. As with public behaviors, the ethical issues are further compounded when the identity of the participant is known by the investigator or could be uncovered by persons who gain access to the investigator's records.

The further danger exists when participant investigators become personally involved in the goals and activities of groups they are investigating and when this involvement causes them to exert undue influence on the group's behavior and to lose objectivity in interpreting data. Investigators involved in participant observation should be particularly sensitive to these issues and should consult regularly on the progress of the investigation and the nature of their involvement with knowledgeable colleagues who are uninvolved in the research.

Some critics feel that the investigator who invades private situations under false pretenses or with concealed observation is entirely out of bounds; others feel that there are circumstances that warrant such behavior. The ethical investigator will assume responsibility for undertaking a study involving covert observation in private situations only after very careful consideration and consultation. Rigorous safeguards of confidentiality may mitigate, but cannot eliminate, the ethical dilemma of an investigator whose scientific goals encourage invading the privacy of others.

Adding research manipulations to existing nonresearch operations in institutional or action research. Persons may find themselves in everyday situations upon which a research component is superimposed: for example, when the relative merits of different textbooks or curricular approaches are evaluated after they have been used in a school district; when an ongoing therapeutic situation is observed to evaluate a therapeutic method; in military research, when different training methods are compared; or in social-action research, when different strategies of family support are studied. To the extent that the research aspect has little or no effect on what participants actually experience and to the extent that the procedures are indigenous to the environment in which the research is conducted, the question arises whether informing participants of the research is necessary. How should we choose between the desirability of informing them and the probability that doing so will have behavioral effects that result in invalid inferences?

The principle of informed consent would rule that there is an obligation to inform individuals of their research roles if there is more than minimal risk; however, the importance of this information to the participant may be minimal, and strong, countervailing, scientific, and practical reasons may exist for not so informing the individuals. Insofar as the research involves comparisons of reasonable variations in the normal program of organizations, there would seem to be no compelling case for insisting absolutely on the informed consent of the participants. Where more than minimal risk is involved, perhaps through lack of anonymity, or where the experimental variation otherwise exceeds "normal" bounds, however, the investigator is not absolved of ethical responsibility by any relationship to the organizations. Whenever participants lack the protection of voluntary consent, the investigator is under special obligation to decide whether the proposed procedures are ethically acceptable.

Obtaining information from third parties. Sometimes the only sources of information about individuals for a particular study are their friends, teachers, acquaintances, counselors, or employers. Problems related to informed consent arise when contact with third parties discloses information to which the participants might object. The procedure may reveal facts or presumptions about research participants that the third-party respondent had not known and thus may violate confidentiality (see Principle J).

Under ideal arrangements, the researcher should obtain the participant's permission to solicit data from third parties. Obtaining such permission may not be possible, however, when the individual cannot be located or for some reason is incompetent to give informed consent. In such cases the investigator should proceed only when responsible analysis of the ethical situation and advice from consultants indicate that the interests of the individual are protected and that the scientific merit of the project is sufficient to warrant the ethical compromise. Having made this decision, the investigator then has the same obligations with respect to the third party that would otherwise pertain to the target individual. The most important of these obligations are obtaining informed consent (Principle D) and maintaining confidentiality (Principle J).

2. Deception.

The foregoing discussion has explored the ways concealment sets limitations on the informed consent of participants and thus results in an ethical dilemma for the investigator who finds it necessary or desirable for scientific reasons to conceal some aspects of the research. The ethical issue is that research participants are uninformed about one or more aspects of the research. Other issues arise when the participants are misinformed—that is, when deception is employed with respect to the purposes of the study or to the meaning of the participant's behavior.

Investigators who have considered the problems raised by deception differ sharply in their conclusions with respect to its use in behavioral research. Many of them treat deception as a particularly serious instance of the more general problem of informed consent. For them, the issue is to be resolved by the same responsible weighing of scientific merit and ethical considerations that has been recommended in the preceding discussion. Other investigators, however, regard deception as an ethical issue of a qualitatively different nature and hold that maintaining open and honest relationships with other human beings and avoiding deceptive and manipulative relationships constitute ethical absolutes. Whatever position investigators take on the issue, they have the responsibility to take cognizance of widespread objections to deception in all human interactions. To remind the investigator of this ethical necessity, the problem of deception has been made the particular focus of Principle E.

The use of deception may serve the scientific purposes of some research. Certain features of the research may be misrepresented because of the belief that an honest representation would adversely affect the potential participant's decision to participate. Having secured an individual's participation, the investigator may need to use deception to disguise a particular procedure or to conceal the meaning of reactions. Even at the end of the experiment leaving participants misinformed may be better than revealing certain aspects of the study. In each of these instances, Principle D puts the investigator in a serious ethical dilemma: Psychologists cannot pursue research involving deception without some compromise of this guideline.

Since the problem is so difficult, investigators should seek advice before proceeding with a study that involves deception. Moreover, it seems advisable for investigators to consult with people whose values differ on the issue of the scientific and ethical justification for deception. Considerations that may make the use of deception more acceptable include the following: (a) The research objective is of great importance and cannot be achieved without the use of deception; (b) on being fully informed later (Principle E), participants are expected to find the procedures reasonable and to suffer no loss of confidence in the integrity of the investigator or of others involved; (c) research participants are allowed to withdraw from the study at any time (Principle F), and are free to withdraw their data when the concealment or misrepresentation is revealed (Principle H); and (e) investigators take full responsibility for detecting and removing stressful aftereffects of the experience (Principle I).

The following discussion focuses on problems associated with the use of deception to secure participation and to achieve desired effects of certain experimental procedures. The discussion of the removal of deception ("debriefing") appears in a later section on the postexperimental treatment of research participants (pages 62–68).

Deception to obtain agreement to participate. An investigator who is well acquainted with a research setting is usually aware of considerations that would lead potential research participants to refuse to cooperate. Thus there is a great temptation to employ misleading information to alleviate the problem. The investigator may purposely fail to mention that the study requires a considerable commitment of time or that its sponsorship may be controversial (e.g., by an organization with particular goals). False expectations about the events to occur may also be created. The ethical burden on the investigator who decides to go ahead with such research is considerable but no different in kind or mode of resolution from dilemmas where important scientific values are in conflict with other important human values. As in other such conflicts, the situation puts the investigator in the position of weighing the pros and cons of doing or radically redesigning the study securing ethical guidance and arriving at a difficult and ambiguous personal decision. Given the lack of consensus on this issue, it is not possible to offer clear-cut guidelines that would be accepted by all psychologists as a way of resolving the ethical dilemmas created by the use of deception. Before doing a study, investigators should ask themselves the general question: "Is this study important enough to warrant the use of deception?" Part of this question can be answered by making sure that the answer is "yes" to certain subsidiary questions: Is an important theoretical question at issue? Is the experimental design sound? Does the manipulation have the effect demanded by the problem under investigation? Will research participants be allowed to discontinue participation at any time or to withdraw their data? Is there access to the resources and the facilities needed to handle adverse consequences should they arise?

Ensuring Freedom from Coercion to Participate (Principle F)

This section deals with the extent to which it is ethically acceptable to bring pressure upon people to participate in psychological research. Freedom is not complete in most areas of life; one is usually constrained by the competing rights and interests of others. But freedom of choice has a value of its own. The need for freedom from coercion becomes increasingly significant to the extent that participation in research entails risks or costs of any type to the participant. Principle F attempts to capture this ideal and, at the same time, to recognize the complexities that are discussed further in this and the following sections.

Principle F. *The investigator respects the individual's freedom to decline to participate in or to withdraw from the research at any time. The obligation to protect this freedom requires careful thought and consideration when the investigator is in a position of authority or influence over the participant. Such positions of authority include, but are not limited to, situations in which research participation is required as part of employment or in which the participant is a student, client, or employee of the investigator.*

The use of coercive measures to obtain the cooperation of participants in research is widespread. "Subject pools" consisting of all of the students enrolled in certain psychology courses exist in many universities. Employees in business and industry are required to participate in research under conditions where they might perceive refusal as placing their jobs in jeopardy. The participation of military personnel may be required under circumstances that virtually rule out resistance.

With regard to extreme positions on the dimension of coerciveness, most people would agree that it would be unethical for an investigator doing research in a prison setting to force prisoners to submit to a highly dangerous research manipulation on the threat that failing to comply would put the prisoner's chance of being paroled in jeopardy (and in fact, this type of coercion is now prohibited by federal regulation and several of state laws). By contrast, almost no one would regard as unethical inducing a college student to take part in a typical memory experiment by offering the student payment for an hour's participation.

The worrisome examples fall between these extremes. To illustrate, even so conventional an incentive as money may become unduly coercive. For example, a prisoner without money might agree to participate in a hazardous experiment for a very small sum. In this case, is the exploitation of the prisoner's special situation not unethical? Would diminishing the prisoner's freedom by withholding the opportunity also be unethical? To consider another example, how coercive is threatening a patient with the denial of therapy for refusing to take part in an experimental study of the effectiveness of the therapeutic agent? Denial of a desperately needed service is generally seen as reprehensible; but is it not appropriate to make research participation a condition of obtaining such a service?

So far only a few of the inducements that are used to motivate research participation have been mentioned. The range of such inducements is, of course, quite wide. Besides financial and other material rewards, moral appeals, such as promising individuals the satisfaction of knowing that they have contributed to the advancement of science or to the solution of social problems, are used. Appeals may be made on the basis of friendship, the positive value of cooperation, or the special needs of the investigator. Is such moral suasion ever unduly coercive? To what extent is it permissible to use social pressure or statements that refusal to participate is a sign of uncooperativeness, lack of courage, and the like?

The problem of coercion sometimes arises even with persons who initially have no objection to taking part in the research. Having agreed to participate, they may find the procedures painful, threatening, or more boring or time consuming than anticipated. Freedom from undue pressure to participate should not end at the start of the experiment. Does a research participant surrender freedom of choice after deciding to participate or does such freedom continue to exist in the form of the option to drop out of the research at any point? Is the researcher ever permitted to impose a penalty for dropping out? If the person does not complete participation, may the investigator withhold all or part of the promised payment? How far is the researcher obliged to go in bringing the opportunity to drop out to the participant's attention? To what extent and by what means might it be permissible to urge a reluctant participant to continue because, for example, allowing participants to drop out might bias the data?

The considerations above identify the degree of risk, the method of coercion, and the extent of coercion as factors to be considered; other factors are the spread of risk and the nature of the relationship of the potential subject to the organization, institution, or society that forms the immediate context of the research. Indeed, coercion usually occurs through an exercise of power in the context of an organization, institution, or society. We shall discuss particular organizational contexts by two brief procedural points.

1. Inmates of Mandatory Total Institutions.

Virtually all the activities and conditions of inmates in correctional facilities, hospitals, and other institutions with in-patient facilities are regulated. Thus the greatest opportunity for compromise with the ideal of free consent occur in these settings. Research is incidental to the main institutional activity, which in turn may be organized in ways that tend to minimize individual freedom of action. The generally coercive character of such institutions may diminish the salience of the more specifically coercive aspect of research participation. Yet research goes on in these settings, and ethical questions arise because patients and prisoners may be required to participate in research without a realistic option to refuse.

How does Principle F apply in these instances? Are the ethical rules governing incentives to participate independent of time and place, or does the institutional setting affect what pressures are permissible? For example, in therapeutic situations, are persons' expectations so different from what they are in academic settings or public places that pressures to participate may be used in the former that would be inadmissible in the latter? When research is conducted without the full voluntary consent of the participants, the decision to do so is commonly justified in terms of the value of the research to institutional objectives. Thus, it is argued, patients should be willing to participate in studies to produce better forms of therapy.

From the perspective of the research participant (for example, an adjudicated mentally disabled patient), however, the goals of the institution may be irrelevant or even objectionable. How are the different views of the individual and the organization to be balanced?

In considering this question it is helpful to distinguish

among three broad types of research occurring in the situations in question. The first is the type in which some aspect of the program of the institution or organization is being evaluated in the hope of improving its effectiveness. The second type is that in which the research topic is concerned with persons in a given setting—but may or may not affect their welfare or that of others like them. The third type is research that takes advantage of the availability of persons who are in the setting (for example, prisoners) but which is no more related to the activities, concerns, or disabilities of these persons than it is to those of people outside the setting.

The first of these three types of research presents the fewest problems. As already noted, research participation that is incidental to systematic study of the effects of normal variations in a regular institutional program appears not to raise serious ethical concerns even when the principle of informed consent is compromised. Thus, just as the effectiveness of alternative curricula may legitimately be studied in educational research without explicit informed permission of students and their parents (other safeguards being observed), so may different policies of ward management be compared. The ethical compromise is similar in the two cases, and, to many, will seem clearly warranted. The safeguard of ethical consultation to protect the interests of the participants become especially important when such a compromise is made. This consideration seems particularly important when major departures from standard programs for improvement and rehabilitation are employed. In such cases, the investigator incurs a special responsibility to ensure the later provision of such benefits as the research participant may have been deprived of in the course of the research (Principle I). The coercive implications of the power relations between participant and staff in these settings is a further reason for exceptional care in protecting the participants' interests.

The second of the three types of research, that requiring the participation of persons like those found in a given institutional setting, raises issues that are harder to resolve. For example, staff research psychologists in a prison or a mental hospital feel an obligation to advance knowledge as it applies to the treatment of persons in their institution. It is easy to understand that this sense of obligation will enter into the investigators' own accounting of the costs and benefits of the research being considered. Not surprisingly, such investigators often feel free to use strong incentives to induce potential participants to take part in the research.

More strongly, some persons may hold that prisoners and patients should be required to cooperate in therapeutic or corrective programs oriented toward their own rehabilitation and, by extension, in research toward improving the program. A difficulty with this position is that it is too readily available as a rationalization for exploitation. On occasion, the institutions in question may serve more to incarcerate and punish than to rehabilitate. Under such circumstances, the argument just presented may lose its force.

Awareness of the justifications and situational factors just discussed is a first step in protecting oneself against practices that show less than full respect for the dignity of the potential research participant. It is important to remember that persons, who from the investigator's or the institution's point of view should cooperate in research, may feel no such obligation. To the contrary, as noted on page 43, such persons may even see the proposed research as operating to their disadvantage, for example, causing discomfort, reducing privileges, or taking time. Such considerations raise serious questions about the use of altruistic or public service incentives in recruiting participants for such research. Granted that there is a real conflict about the use of such incentives in recruiting research participants, can any suggestions be offered to deal with the dilemma? From one point of view, according to Principle F, the investigator must respect the potential participants' freedom to decline participation. Moreover, as Principle F also says, the investigator's position of power with respect to the participant requires special care to protect that freedom.

From another point of view, however, Principle F does not imply that investigators are constrained from communicating to members of the target population a sense of the possible value of the proposed research and the need, as investigators see it, for cooperation. For the investigator to so communicate with conviction without at the same time bringing to bear the power associated with a staff position admittedly will be difficult. What must be attempted is to provide potential participants with a meaningful argument that their participation may help solve a serious problem without at the same time implying disapproval or punishment for refusal to take part.

In the third type of research, that without any special relationship either to the program in the special setting or to the characteristics of persons in that setting, the ethical dilemma takes a different form. In such research the argument that the potential participant is under some obligation to take part can no longer be made. Accordingly, the focus shifts to the kind and strength of incentives the investigator is warranted in using. One precaution is strongly recommended: When potential research participants have such strong needs that they have little real freedom to reject incentives related to these needs, an investigator should never use such incentives without first securing ethical advice from consultants.

2. Clients of Non-Mandatory Service Organizations.

In many instances the client has some choice of the service used and its source. For example, several out-patient or educational facilities may be available and the option to refuse service may exist. Within educational institutions there is a choice of sections, courses, and curricula. The existence of these choices limits the opportunity for coercion. One must, however, accurately assess the extent of choice and carefully choose research procedures that are appropriate to it. If the service is in short supply, the users (for example, students of limited means) may be vulnerable. Indeed, there is such concern about the forced participation of students in research—the "subject pool"—that the following guidelines are suggested.

a. Students are informed about the research requirement before they enroll in the course, typically by an announcement in an official listing of courses. In addition, during the first class meeting, the instructor provides a detailed description of the requirement, frequently in written form, covering the following points: the amount of participation required; the available alternatives to actual research participation; in a general way, the kinds of studies among which the student can choose; the right of the student to drop out of a given research project at any time without penalty; any penalties to be imposed for failure to complete the requirement or for nonappearance after agreeing to take part; the benefits to the student to be gained from participation; the obligation of the researcher to provide the student with an explanation of the research; the obligation of the researcher to treat the participant with respect and dignity; the procedures to be followed if the student is mistreated in any way; and an explanation of the scientific purposes of the research carried on in the departmental laboratories.

b. Prior approval of research proposals, sometimes by a single faculty member but more often by a departmental committee or an Institutional Review Board, is recommended. The following considerations are appropriate for the review:

Will dangerous or potentially harmful procedures be employed? If so, what precautions have been taken to protect the participants from the possibly damaging effects of the procedure? Will inordinate demands be made upon the participants' time? Will the research involve deception or withholding information? If so, what plans have been developed for subsequently informing the participants? What plans have been made for providing the participants with an explanation of the study? In general, what will the participants gain?

c. Alternative opportunities for research participation are provided. This provision lets students choose the type of research experience and (often of more consequence to students) the time and place where they will participate.

Providing options commensurate in time and effort that do not require service as a research participant is necessary.

The student may observe ongoing research and prepare a report based upon this experience or submit a short paper based upon the reading of research reports. Care should be taken to ensure that selecting such options has no punitive consequences.

d. Before beginning participation, the student receives a description of the procedures to be employed and is reminded of the option to drop out later without penalty if so desired. At this point consent is sought, and the student may be asked to document consent in writing. In any event, participation in any teacher's own research project should be optional for all students.

e. Steps are taken to ensure that the participant is treated with respect and courtesy.

f. Participants receive some kind of reward for their participation. At a minimum this reward involves as full an explanation of the purposes of the research as is possible. In addition, some departments may reward research participation with better grades, although many critics would question the educational propriety of this practice. The assignment of a grade of "incomplete" as a sanction against nonfulfillment is common, although some critics regard this as too coercive. Where this sanction is used, procedures exist for allowing the student to fulfill the requirement later.

g. There is a mechanism by which students may report any mistreatment. Usually the mechanism involves reporting questionable conduct on the part of an investigator to the instructor, the departmental ethics committee, or the chair of the department.

h. The recruiting procedure is under constant review. Assessments of student attitudes toward the requirement are obtained at the end of each course having such a requirement each time the course is offered. These data, together with evaluations of the workability of the procedures by the investigators, provide the basis for modifying the procedures in subsequent years.

Conclusion. The discussion above applies only to the use of a research participation requirement for recruitment in studies that, although often nonpedagogical in character, do offer the participant a potential educational gain. When, as is sometimes the case, the latter feature is missing, the investigator should consider the possibility of using other means of recruiting research participants. The ethical sense of this point is widely recognized. In studies that require many hours of participation, the educational gain to the student is often exhausted early in the investigation. In such cases, the common practice is to pay the participants for their services. Where educational gains are available to the student, procedures like those discussed here do much to ensure compliance with Principle F and the other principles set forth in this document.

3. The Participant as a Service Provider.

Unlike students and inmates of therapeutic or correctional institutions, some individuals become potential participants in research because of their role as employees or paid service providers. In some cases, the employers or users of the services take steps to ensure that the services are appropriately delivered, as through training, supervision, and the implementation of prerequisites for promotion and hiring; as with other industrial processes, the effectiveness of various aspects of these processes must be evaluated for efficient management. These generally accepted steps require the participation of the service provider. When the number of such service providers is large, as in a large organization, or when the instances of a particular service are many, a systematic and scientific (i.e., research) approach to the management of the services is needed. This research is conducted in a context where the indifference of service providers to organizational or client objectives must be differently regarded than would be, for example, the prisoner's lack of interest in the goals of the corrective facility. Competing, legitimate interests exist, and the service provider recognizes them as a condition of employment. The use of research procedures to operate large personnel systems and to improve the effectiveness of such systems, for example, has become so pervasive that one would be hard pressed to suppose that research participation is not expected. Because of that expectation, it is desirable that a clear and fair statement of the expectation of participation in management research and the general consequences of participation be included in the employment agreement. Clearly, one cannot anticipate all the studies that might be needed, but an establishment of the limits of risk should be possible. The existence of these competing interests underscores the necessity for careful consideration when the influence and authority that result from the investigator's relationship to the sponsoring organization are used. Projects can be formulated so that the participants' dignity and welfare are not at stake. Care can be taken so that records that would not exist except for the research do not find their way into the personnel files. Clearly, it is absolutely necessary that the projects involved bear directly and immediately on questions whose answers in turn directly affect the enterprises involved, that the projects be subject to extra rigors of quality of design, and that the sponsoring agencies have a clear plan and intention for the use of the results. Projects implemented only for political purposes and projects that bear broadly but not directly on organizational operation and projects undertaken because of the conveniences of a captive sample are not suggested as examples where the competing interests have any application. The material on pages entitled Ethical Issues in the Sponsorship of Research should also be considered.

Employees in the private sector are service providers in the sense of interest here, but so are those in the public sector, including the military, at least in the all-volunteer environment, where in peacetime the competing interests are not so apparent. But the military services exist for conditions involving risk, coercion, and, for some, death. To preclude research inquiry into combat-related matters under peacetime conditions, where stress and risk can be humanely controlled, would seem to be an unnecessarily harsh concentration of risk on those in the service during wartime. But allowing withdrawal of research subjects at any time would likely preclude adequate variation of experimental conditions (although one could first try the study allowing withdrawal) and would produce the undesirable concentration. In this context, emphasizing the cautions of the paragraph above seems appropriate. The projects should bear clearly and immediately on the capacity of the organization to function, and there should be a clear plan and intention to use the results; otherwise, little spreading of risk can occur. In addition, the use of a recruiting agreement that incorporates a clear statement of expectations with respect to participation in research, tests, and evaluation is extremely desirable.

Finally, certain individuals exist outside of the context of employment by an organization but provide services so that the state, on behalf of its citizens, has an interest in their performance. As with employees, the rights of those who profit through receiving licensure or certification are subject to competing claims from their benefactors, the public, as represented by the state. Research on the licensing system might be needed to improve its effectiveness, for example, on the quality of services provided or on the balance of quality of service and available suppliers of service, as moderated by the licensure/certification system in force. As with employment, an investigator conducting research on licensing and certification systems has the responsibility to protect the service-provider subjects; but, with such protection, it is reasonable to expect cooperation from the licensee.

 4. Clarity of the Person's Right to Refuse or Discontinue Participation.

Questions often arise as to whether the person's opportunity to refuse to participate or to drop out after participation has begun is made sufficiently clear. Special problems arise when the demand characteristics of a situation are such as to make refusal or dropping out difficult. Other questions arise in connection with certain types of people or with certain states of mind. Whatever the circumstances, the conflict of the investigator derives from the fact that refusal to participate or to continue participation diminishes the representativeness of the sample of research participants. To what extent should the investigator allow such considerations to limit these options?

Problems arise concerning the clarity of the person's right to refuse participation when the individual is in a relationship of dependency with the researcher that might interfere with the exercising of the right to refuse. The teacher-student, doctor-patient, and employer-employee relationships are examples. One possible resolution to many problems of this type is to protect the prospective participant's right to refuse by turning over the recruitment of participants and the conduct of the research to a third party not involved in the relationship. Such precautions should help to protect the person's right both to refuse to participate and to drop out later. When the person has strong reasons to refuse to participate and a coercive element remains, the investigator is obliged to take precautions to ensure that the research is warranted and that the participant's interests are protected. This kind of problem is considered further in the section dealing with fairness and freedom from exploitation in the research relationship (pages 30–34).

5. The Participant's Right to Withdraw Data.

Although Principle F does not specifically mention the right of the participants to withdraw their data from a study after participation is otherwise completed, there are cases where the discontinuance of participation may take this form. This possibility becomes important when, for sufficient reasons, the investigator has found it necessary to withhold or distort information that is relevant to the participant's informed consent to participate (see pages 41–42).

In research employing deception in which the investigator subsequently explains the purposes and procedures of the study, the participant should be given the explicit opportunity to withdraw the data. In the more usual situation in which the participant's genuinely informed consent has been obtained prior to participation, spontaneous wishes to withdraw data should be respected; but the investigators are under no special obligation to raise the issue at the end of the research session.

Protection From Discomfort, Harm, and Danger (Principle G)

In most psychological research, the participants are exposed neither to appreciable physical suffering or danger nor to appreciably stressful conditions. The relatively rare studies involving physical harm or danger are typically undertaken to clarify important topics such as motivation or the nature of pain and its relief. The investigator may be studying the stressful state itself as an essential aspect of the research (e.g., the effects of drugs on pain suppression) or may be using deprivation, electric shock, or intense noise to manipulate motivational or incentive conditions.

Likewise, a stressful procedure may be the essential independent variable, as when the investigator exposes participants to varying levels of failure in order to study the effects of loss of self-esteem on ways of coping or to temptations to lie or cheat in order to study moral functioning and development. In other studies, the discomfort or stressful procedure may involve a less essential aspect of the research, as when different levels of anxiety are induced in order to study the effects of drive level on stimulus generalization. In still other cases, the stressful conditions may arise incidentally or accidentally, as when some participants are embarrassed by certain questionnaire items in ways difficult to anticipate or when the participant unexpectedly develops feelings of having done poorly on a learning task.

Responsible investigators obviously would not expose research participants to actual or potential physical or psychological harm if there were not a very serious reason for doing so. Although some psychologists believe that such research should be entirely prohibited, the dominant view in the field is probably that when such studies are important, they should be continued. Under what circumstances is research involving discomfort, harm, or danger permissible?

Studies that raise this question are relatively rare partly because investigators are ingenious enough to find alternate ways of studying the research problem at issue. For example, much research on deprivation employs nonhuman animals, uses deprivations or procedures that are relatively trivial in type and amount, or studies persons who are undergoing differential amounts of deprivation or are exposed to stressful conditions of varying degrees for reasons independent of the research and beyond the investigator's control. Where such alternatives cannot be found, however, the importance of the research must be measured against the appreciable costs to the participant. When the investigator decides that research involving physical or mental stress is warranted, what measures should be taken to protect the welfare of the participants?

Investigators may find themselves in conflict between the obligation to carry out research they feel might yield important human benefits and the obligation to avoid treating research participants in ways likely to harm them or to expose them to appreciably stressful conditions. In resolving these conflicting obligations, investigators must weigh the degree of stressful circumstances that will be involved and the number of participants who will be exposed to the experience against the possible benefits that the research might yield. Research involving stressful conditions or risk of physical or psychological harm may be conducted only for highly important purposes and only after a thorough search for alternatives to minimize danger or discomfort. A decision that such a study is ethically warranted requires that safeguards to protect the participant be commensurate with the stressful circumstances or risk of harm. Such a decision may be reached responsibly only after full technical and ethical consultation. Principle G summarizes the investigator's responsibilities. It implies that the principles relating to informed consent to participate (Principle D), to fairness and freedom from exploitation in the research relationship (Principle F), and to removal of stressful consequences following completion of the research (Principle I) must be scrupulously observed—with compromise in these principles not to be tolerated insofar as the stressful or risky circumstances are serious.

Principle G. ***The investigator protects the participant from physical and mental discomfort, harm, and danger that may arise from research procedures. If risks of such consequences exist, the investigator informs the participant of that fact. Research procedures likely to cause serious or lasting harm to a participant are not used unless the failure to use these procedures might expose the participant to risk of greater harm or unless the research has great potential benefit and fully informed and voluntary consent is obtained from each participant. The participant should be informed of procedures for contacting the investigator within a reasonable time period following participation should stress, potential harm, or related questions or concerns arise.***

Because the specific contexts of ethical decision differ for physical and for psychological discomfort, harm, and danger, the two situations will be discussed separately.

Physical Discomfort, Harm, and Danger
1. Types of Research That Involve Physical Discomfort, Harm, and Danger.

In some types of behavioral research, the occurrence of appreciable physical discomfort is certain. Studying various aspects of pain (including its physiological basis, determinants of its intensity, or ways of ameliorating it), for example, is likely to involve exposing participants to pain. In other research, physical discomfort is centrally—if less essentially—involved as a way of manipulating the participant's motivation. For example, the participant is deprived of food or water for appreciable periods, or punishment such as electric shock or loud noise is used to eliminate erroneous responses. Other studies expose the participants to unpleasant tastes, extreme temperatures, or other special states that are likely to produce pain or discomfort. Obtaining certain kinds of physiological indices also entails some degree of pain or discomfort. For example, obtaining blood samples, which might be quite tolerable to most participants, may be highly disturbing to a few.

One type of research that deserves special mention is the administration of drugs that have a high likelihood of causing appreciable adverse effects. Besides raising issues comparable to those mentioned above, drugs involve additional dangers such as the possibility of causing addiction and violating legal regulations. Thus special problems arise in obtaining informed consent while yet avoiding spurious suggestion effects by giving information about the drug.

There are several other conditions in which serious danger or discomfort is much less likely to occur but remains a worrisome possibility because of unanticipated accidents, equipment failures, or the involvement of particularly susceptible participants. Included here would be such procedures as cardiac conditioning, inducement of high levels of fatigue, or use of recording techniques that may produce anxiety because they are not fully understood by the participant. Investigators must be sufficiently familiar with their areas of work to appreciate such unlikely but serious possibilities, take measures to lessen their likelihood, and anticipate what is to be done if they occur. These issues are considered more fully in subsequent sections.

2. Alternative Procedures to Avoid Physical Discomfort, Harm, and Danger.

To the extent that research involves the likelihood of physical discomfort or danger, the investigator is obligated to search for substitute techniques that might avoid such experiences. One possibility is the use of nonhuman animals instead of humans, as is frequently done in studies of deprivation and aversive stimulation. One is obliged to treat lower animals humanely, but current ethical standards usually permit a higher level of physical risk to nonhuman animals in important research.

Some studies to ascertain the effectiveness of a new treatment involve using a control group that is deprived of a possible benefit, for example, a "placebo" group to test the benefits of a new drug. The investigator contemplating such a design might consider lessening the deprivation of the control group by giving them a treatment of known effectiveness rather than no treatment.

Some research may be conducted by studying persons undergoing stressful conditions as part of their inevitable life experiences, so that the investigator need not inflict physical discomfort. An investigator interested in ascertaining ways of ameliorating pain through the use of hypnosis, for example, might avoid the use of pain-inflicting procedures by selecting participants who are already experiencing unavoidable pain because of therapeutic procedures, illness, or the like. However, ethical problems do arise when the investigator, for research purposes, allows such stress-producing situations to continue by withholding possible alleviating treatments.

When some level of physical discomfort is judged to be necessary and tolerable in order to study a sufficiently significant problem, the investigator should be careful to keep the discomfort at a minimum. Even when using electric shock, aversive noise levels, and the like is judged permissible, the levels should be set sufficiently low, on the basis of pretests and personal participation, so that the experience would not be intolerable even to the more sensitive participants among those who pass a careful screening procedure.

3. Safety Precautions to Minimize Possible Dangers to the Participants.

The investigator's obligation is to be fully informed about the possible dangers involved in any of the procedures used. Some procedures involve sufficiently clear and present dangers so that any reasonable investigator will perceive the need for a number of precautions. For example, even when special circumstances may justify the administration of electric shocks to adequately informed and freely consenting participants, the investigator obviously owes the participant the taking of a variety of precautions. The investigators and any assistants should be thoroughly familiar with the physical and physiological factors involved in electric shocks and with the particular apparatus used. They must ensure that the equipment is in a state that precludes dangerous shock levels. Moreover, the investigators must ascertain that the participants do not suffer from any special conditions that would make the levels of shocks to be used in any way dangerous to them. Also, the investigators must consider emergencies that might arise and make appropriate preparations to deal with them.

In the case of other treatments with potential dangers comparable to that of administering electric shocks, investigators should take similarly appropriate safety precautions including training of the personnel, pretesting of the equipment, screening the participants, and making emergency plans to deal with accidents. Even with seemingly innocuous procedures, the investigator's responsibility is to anticipate accidents and to take appropriate safety precautions.

4. Screening Susceptible Participants in Research Involving Physical Discomfort or Danger.

Where special circumstances lead to the judgment that exposing participants to physical discomfort or danger is permissible, eliminating certain classes of people from the pool of participants is usually necessary. For example, studies of pain that might be judged permissible with fully informed and freely volunteering adults would be judged unsuitable for children because children might be less familiar with and, therefore, terrified by such experiences or because their fundamental trust might be violated. Again, it would be inappropriate to use patients or other clients who depend for services upon the institution sponsoring the research (e.g., mentally disabled persons, elderly people, or hospitalized patients) because they might not adequately appreciate that participation is voluntary and strictly for research nor understand the discomfort likely to be experienced.

Even with the normal adult population, the investigator must be aware of the wide range of individual differences in susceptibility to the discomforts and dangers involved in various physically stressful procedures. Unrecognized physical defects or allergies, for example, might make a seemingly healthy individual particularly susceptible to an experimental drug or particularly sensitive to some type of discomfort-causing stimulus. The investigator, therefore, is obliged to be familiar with such conditions that heighten susceptibility and to recognize and screen out of the research those people who have such conditions. For example, a study of substance abuse that varies the dose well within limits deemed appropriate for most persons might be completely unacceptable for people with drug-related problems. That is, for such individuals, free and informed consent is not enough; the investigator should be aware that the very enthusiasm of some persons to take part in such research may be symptomatic of their problem and therefore requires excluding them from the study.

5. Dangerous Research Treatments Benefiting the Participant.

The investigator must be especially careful not to expose certain classes of people, such as children and patients, to considerable physical discomfort or danger solely for research purposes. However, exposing persons to stressful conditions solely for research purposes should be distinguished from doing research in situations where therapeutic or diagnostic procedures are used for the possible benefit of the participants themselves. Here the major consideration is the justifiability of procedures that involve additional physical discomfort or pain only for research purposes. Although the diagnostician or therapist should be cautious in the use of dangerous procedures, even for the patient's benefit, it may be reasonable to allow a higher likelihood of adverse effects when the treatment is being employed for the possible benefit of the participant than when it is being employed strictly for research purposes.

6. Necessity for Continued Assurance of Freedom to End Participation at Any Point.

The importance of ensuring that participants take part in research only by their free and informed consent is discussed at a number of places in this document (pages 47, 50–51). The point needs particular emphasis with studies that involve any appreciable physical discomfort or danger. The investigator should be sensitive to subtle pressures that limit participants' effective freedom to decline taking part in the study. For example, in studies involving pain, the investigator should particularly avoid recruitment procedures such as talking the person into participation on the basis of the importance of the work to science or society. In these situations, investigators should try to relieve the person of any negative feelings or self-doubts about refusal to participate. Although it might be difficult for investigators to testify against themselves in the quest for suitable participants, they are obliged to be sensitive to these issues.

Furthermore, the investigator should be especially careful in situations involving physically stressful procedures to ensure that the person remains aware that participation can be terminated at any point. Particularly, there should be no pressure on the individual to continue if reluctance to go on with the study is indicated. But, even more, the investigator should be constantly vigilant for any signs of incipient reluctance by the participant and should make clear during the procedure that termination is possible at any time.

7. Problems Regarding Informed Consent in Research Involving Administration of Drugs and Other Treatments.

In studies on drug effects with human participants, the investigator must control spurious effects resulting from the participant's suggestibility. That is, if fully informed about the nature of the drug and its possible direct or side effects, the participant might experience these effects because of having been told that they might occur rather than because of the chemical action of the drugs. The investigator is thus caught in a conflict of values: Either the research is carried out without obtaining the participant's fully informed consent, or it is carried out with the danger that the fully informed participant might show effects due to suggestion. The latter choice becomes a dilemma because complete honesty about drug tests means that the active medication must overcome a very strong placebo effect prior to being classified as active; thus, honesty to the experimental participant about the placebo may deprive the investigator of an opportunity to distinguish the psychological from the physiological (pharmacological) effect of a drug-taking regimen. Another alternative is to forego the research that might lead to important human benefits.

The responsible investigator must attempt to resolve such a conflict in a way that takes account of the various elements in this dilemma. It may be possible, for example, to withhold some of the specific details about potential effects of the drug, provided that the participant is made aware that drugs are indeed being administered and that they might produce discomforts or dangers of specific magnitude (even if the particular nature of these effects is not made explicit). Then the investigator should, at any time it seems required for the well-being of the participants (and certainly at the end of the study), fully inform the participants of the specific symptoms that might be experienced in connection with the drug.

8. Legal Aspects of Research Involving Administration of Drugs.

Administration of drugs that involve the possibility of discomfort or danger to the recipient raises all the problems considered above inherent in other physically stressful treatments. But there are also legal problems peculiar to drug research. The use of certain drugs even for research purposes is proscribed by law. And in situations where the administration of certain dangerous drugs is legal in research contexts, often legal restrictions or obligations that raise special dangers of criminal penalties to the institutions or the participants are imposed on the investigator. Hence, investigators planning to administer drugs as part of a research project should make certain they have observed the appropriate legal safeguards. At a minimum, it is important to ascertain that the drug has been obtained legally, used under conditions specified by federal and state laws, and tested appropriately. As in all drug studies with human beings, the investigator should be familiar with the known effects of the drug and conduct the research with whatever medical collaboration is prescribed by the law.

Finally, investigators studying illegal drug use should be especially mindful that the requirements of anonymity and confidentiality apply in their studies with a special force, for there might well be situations in which information obtained from participants about their use of illegal drugs is requested by law enforcement agencies. The drug researcher should be particularly sensitive to this possibility and when obtaining consent to participate, should make clear to the participants the extent to which their anonymity and the confidentiality of the data will be protected in the face of legal demands. (See Principle J on the protection of confidentiality.)

Psychological Discomfort, Harm, and Danger

1. Types of Behavioral Research in Which Psychological Discomfort, Harm, or Danger May Occur.

As in any situation involving human relations, insulting and thoughtless behavior on the part of the investigator may distress the participants. The present discussion deals not with such negligence or crudeness on the part of investigators—which is reprehensible—but with situations in which the research procedures cause the participants psychological distress, either as an essential part of the investigation, as an incidental part, or as an accidental side effect.

In some psychological studies, the essential independent variables involve stressful procedures. For example, participants are exposed to failure experiences, to opportunities and temptations to lie, cheat, steal, or inflict suffering on others, and to sexually arousing materials or scenes of extreme human suffering. Participants may be asked to reveal personal data they find embarrassing or to perform disturbing tasks such as rating their parents. In still other studies the distress is caused inadvertently, as when the experience proves more disturbing or tedious than the investigator anticipated.

The investigator's obligation is to determine whether the study might be appreciably distressing to the participant; if such distress seems likely, the research should be stopped unless there is compelling reason to continue. That is, it must be ascertained that the importance of the research justifies the degree of exposure to stressful conditions; and, where possible, the informed participant as well as the investigator must agree that such is the case. In addition, the investigator is obliged to minimize the degree and the duration of such discomfort.

2. Monitoring for Unintended Stressful Conditions.

Any reasonable investigator will be aware that certain types of experimental studies likely will result in appreciable discomfort for the participants. Also, one must recognize that a variety of other research procedures might accidentally prove to be psychologically stressful or traumatic. Likewise, participants sometimes are more vulnerable than the investigator has anticipated; for example, participants may conclude on the basis of their performance on a memory task that they have done very poorly and thus are inadequate. (See Principles H and I, pages 62–68.) In other studies, participants may be disturbed at being asked certain questions that the investigator has assumed are quite innocuous; for example, the investigator might fail to anticipate that asking some children from fatherless homes to state the name of father and mother might prove a stressful and embarrassing task.

3. Substitutes for Employing Stressful Procedures.

Experienced investigators who work on important problems that involve stressful experiences have demonstrated that these problems can be studied using naturally occurring conditions. For example, rather than employing stressful procedures it is sometimes possible to study individuals in unavoidable, naturally occurring, stressful circumstances. Illustrative examples include observation of students before and after important examinations and persons awaiting their turn in the dentist's chair. Ethical problems arise when the use of such occasions for research involves the participant in morally unacceptable situations. There are, of course, problems in selecting subjects and, generally, in studying natural situations.

Other researchers have collected data through phenomenological investigations or role-playing studies in which participants report how they would behave in certain situations (e.g., whether or not they would lie under one or another type of inducement). There are, however, serious questions about the validity of obtained results using these methodologies. Because of the clear need for a better understanding of such important but highly sensitive phenomena, the investigator must weigh the scientific costs of inadequate or misleading results against the moral costs of psychologically stressful procedures.

    4. The Necessity of Minimizing the Degree and Duration of Psychologically Stressful Conditions.

Convinced of the importance of the problem being studied, investigators are naturally inclined to make sure that the independent variable is manipulated sufficiently to permit its effects to be discernible; however, they must balance this inclination against the obligation to protect the research participant from discomfort, harm, and danger.

    5. Special Problems of Obtaining Informed Consent to Participate in Research Employing Psychologically Stressful Procedures.

As indicated in Principle D, the investigator is obligated to employ as participants only those who have freely consented to serve when fully knowledgeable about all aspects of the research experience that might reasonably be expected to influence their decision to participate. If the research involves stressful conditions, the investigator should specify in advance the possibility of discomfort even when details of the stressful experience cannot be revealed. For example, participants must experience failure under circumstances where credibility would be lessened if the investigator warned of the possibility of such failure; or they may be given an opportunity to cheat or steal, supposedly without the investigator's knowledge, so that an advance warning would make the situation less meaningful.

The decision on the part of the investigator to go ahead with a study in which the participants are exposed without prior warning to appreciably stressful conditions raises serious ethical concerns. When the investigator concludes that it is indeed obligatory to proceed without warning the participant, persons more concerned for the participants' well-being than with the progress of the research should be consulted for additional feedback. When the research does proceed, each participant should be carefully interviewed after participation to make sure that the stressful condition is minimized (see Principle I).

    6. Special Problems of Deception in Research Involving Psychologically Stressful Conditions.

The topic of deception in psychological research has been discussed on pages 34–42. Deserving special mention here, however, is an aspect of deception involved in studies where psychologically stressful procedures are used. In some such studies, for example, the procedure consists of forewarning the individual of impending electric shocks when, in fact, there will be none. Data from these experimental participants are then compared with the data from control participants who have not been so deceived. Debriefing sessions that follow such studies subsequently inform the participants about the deceptive nature of the experiment. In other studies the participants are given the impression that they are inflicting punishment on another person who, unknown to them, is actually an actor only pretending to be hurt; at the end of such research, the participants are made aware that the apparatus had been arranged so that they were really not hurting the other person at all.

On one hand, studies such as these, involving deception and psychologically stressful conditions, have been criticized as ethically unacceptable. On the other hand, they have been defended on grounds that they contribute to an improved understanding of fundamental psychological processes and important practical problems. When such studies can be justified, the investigator incurs a strong obligation to minimize possible psychological damage to the research participants.

Previous experience indicates that a simple postinvestigation explanation of the true nature of the study and its procedures may not be sufficient: Some participants may experience greater stressful consequences upon learning of the deception than they had experienced during the actual experiment. The investigator's obligation is to anticipate and ameliorate such reactions at the termination of the study.

7. Revealing Participants' Weaknesses.

In a number of psychological studies, some participants may incidentally learn of their personal weaknesses. In some studies, this awareness comes as an inevitable concomitant of participation. For example, the individuals in an obedience study may discover that they are capable of being quite brutal when so urged by an authority figure; or in a study on moral temptation, the individuals may observe how ready they are to cheat or to lie. In other studies, the painful insight does not come from the participation per se but from the investigator's full disclosure at the end of the research to some of the participants that they did not do particularly well at some task.

Some commentators have argued that truth is intrinsically good; therefore, new insights that research participants may receive into their own true characteristics are positive, desirable benefits. Others argue that, while this logic may be acceptable where positive or welcome insights are concerned, the uninvited and unanticipated presentation to research participants of negative, threatening, or damaging information about themselves is ethically undesirable. This argument runs that, while such insights may be appropriate to a psychotherapeutic relationship, in which such self-disclosure is commonplace and expected, they are not appropriate to the participant–investigator relationship. At the very least, investigators must realize that such revelations are likely to be psychologically stressful. It is necessary, therefore, to anticipate and minimize these effects.

8. Potentially Irreversible Aftereffects.

In some investigations, the potential for negative aftereffects seems especially great, and the possible irreversibility of these aftereffects must be considered. Under such conditions, the investigation obviously should not be conducted.

Responsibilities to Research Participants Following Completion of the Research (Principles H and I)

The investigator has the obligation to ensure that research participants do not leave the research experiencing undesirable aftereffects attributable to their participation. Such negative consequences can arise if steps are not taken to ameliorate painful consequences or even if the participants are permitted to remain confused or misinformed about important aspects of the study.

Clarifying the Nature of the Research to the Participant at the End of the Study (Principle H)

As discussed on pages 34-42, many investigators assert that the best research procedures sometimes necessitate withholding complete information about the study or giving participants certain misconceptions about themselves or about events occurring during the study. In some cases, misconceptions not deliberately induced by the investigator occur during the course of the study.

The responsible investigator is obliged not only to correct at the end of the study any misconceptions that the participant develops during the research but also to provide a full account of facets of the study not revealed during participation. This account may include the full particulars about the problem under investigation, the broader significance of the research, the ways in which the research might contribute to the solution of the problem, and the value of the role played by the participant in this process.

On pages 51–62, the various circumstances that may justify inducing or permitting the occurrence of certain misconceptions during the course of an investigation have been considered in detail. Whenever conditions such as these prevail, the investigator is faced with several difficult questions. For example, are investigators always obligated to check for and correct misconceptions, even if the conditions of their occurrence have not been deliberately arranged? Must the lack of information or the misconceptions be corrected immediately, or may the correction wait until all participants have completed the experiment or until any given participant has completed all the sessions? Must the investigator correct misinformation or provide missing information even when such information will be distressing to the participant? What modifications of usual procedures are required when the research participants are children? These and related questions identify the central concern of this section.

The need to conduct research in a way that makes it maximally informative may cause the investigator to withhold from the participant certain information concerning the design and procedure or even to misinform the participant during the time when data are being actively collected, provided such misinformation does not put the participant at risk. Once this participation is completed, however, reasons for allowing the participant to be uninformed or misinformed generally no longer obtain, and the investigator is obliged to provide full clarification. This clarification is especially important when continuation in the misinformed or uninformed condition might have some deleterious effect on the participant. The longer the uninformed or misinformed condition persists, the greater the likelihood of errors or inappropriate action on the part of the participant. Also, the longer the condition persists, the more likely it is that the subsequent disclosure will have a detrimental impact on the participant's trust in interpersonal relationships. Practically, too, it is often difficult to locate the participant after the study and to secure attendance at a session in which clarification may be presented.

Principle H. *After the data are collected, the investigator provides the participant with information about the nature of the study and attempts to remove any misconceptions that may have arisen. Where scientific or humane values justify delaying or withholding this information, the investigator incurs a special responsibility to monitor the research and to ensure that there are no damaging consequences for the participant.*

The experience of many researchers attests to the fact that one is likely to encounter a number of difficulties and special problems in the effort to implement this principle.

1. Avoiding Angering or Disillusioning the Participants.

When planning an investigation that involves misleading or misinforming research participants, the investigator must be alert to the possibility that the postinvestigation clarification procedure may generate anger or resentment in the research participants. Participants sometimes will be embarrassed at having been deceived so easily or resentful toward the investigator and toward psychological research in general.

The possibility of such deleterious effects of postresearch clarification imposes on the investigator the additional obligation to consider alternative research designs. Moreover, it is essential to develop a clarification procedure that will not only leave the participant fully informed but will also minimize the likelihood of any serious resentment toward the investigator, the institution, or future research. In addition, the investigator should attempt to ensure that the participant will not suffer loss of self-esteem or disillusionment regarding interpersonal trust.

2. Providing Information Regarding the Outcome of a Study After Data Are Analyzed and Interpreted.

Frequently the investigator cannot provide information about the outcome of the study to the participant immediately after the data are collected; however, the participant's appreciation of the research experience may be much improved by providing the full report of the outcome of the research, or at least an abstract of it, as soon as possible after the completion of the study. The investigator should consider the importance of such a report and, if it seems likely to be useful to participants, should collect information (e.g., future addresses) that will allow the report to be forwarded to them. When a promise is made to send such materials, the investigator should honor the obligation.

3. Waiting Until All Participants Have Completed the Study Before Any Are Given Clarification.

In some instances, the investigator may feel it is inadvisable to provide full clarification to any of the participants until data have been collected from all of the participants who will take part in the study, because some of the participants might talk among themselves and convey information that would vitiate the study. Such a development is particularly likely where the participants are drawn from a small population (such as from students on a college campus). In such instances, the participants can be told before they take part in the study that full clarification will be provided after the study is completed.

4. The Multiple-Session Study.

In many psychological studies, the participant must serve in several sessions separated by an interval of time that may extend for days or weeks. Such a study poses a problem if deception, misunderstanding, or discomfort occur in the first session and if providing a full explanation of what happened in that session will vitiate the usefulness of the data collected in the following sessions. For this reason, redesigning the study so that it can be carried out within a single session, with the participant not leaving the laboratory until full clarification is provided, is often desirable.

At other times, the demands of the research may not permit full clarification until the final session is completed. In such cases, the investigator must take into account the possibility that there will be deleterious effects from allowing the person to leave the laboratory misinformed or uninformed and must consider the possibility of altering the research design or even of abandoning the study altogether. In cases where such conflicts arise, it is often useful for the investigator to consult with others, including those who are especially involved in the welfare of the participant, regarding the permissibility of providing the clarification only at the end of several sessions.

 5. Incredulity Regarding the Postinvestigation Clarification.

If the research procedures permit the development of unusually firm misconceptions by the participants, the investigator may encounter the participants' skepticism when postinvestigation clarification is later attempted.

In this case, the investigator must make a strong effort to assure the participant that the postinvestigation clarification is complete and accurate. Usually it is most effective to explain in detail why the participant had to be left ignorant or misinformed during the process of data collection and to show that the circumstances that required the original deception are no longer operative. Furthermore, the investigator should provide the participant with ample opportunity to raise additional questions, which then should be fully, honestly, and convincingly answered. Persisting doubts by participants during "debriefing" raise serious questions, moreover, about the ethical acceptability of the deceptions employed.

There have been a few studies that employ "double deception." This practice involves a second deception presented as part of what the participant thinks is the official postinvestigation clarification procedure. Then some further measurement is made, followed by clarification of the deceptions and procedures. In such cases, there is danger that the participant, when finally provided with a full and accurate clarification, will remain unconvinced and possibly resentful. Hence, such procedures should be avoided if possible.

 6. Lack of Interest on the Part of the Subject.

The investigator occasionally confronts the situation in which the participant is not especially interested in hearing the clarification that the investigator has intended to provide. This occurrence is most likely when the person's consent to participate has been induced by some extraneous consideration, such as financial payment, or when experiences in the study have been of little interest. In such cases, the participant might prefer, if given the choice, to leave rather than to stay and hear the investigator's explanation of the study. The investigator should recognize the participants' preference in such instances.

 7. Special Considerations With Children.

The implementation of Principle H in research with children poses special problems. With children, the primary objective of the postinvestigation clarification procedure is to ensure that the child leaves the research situation with no undesirable aftereffects of participation. Attaining this objective may mean, for example, that certain misconceptions should not be removed or even that some new misconceptions should be induced. If children erroneously believe that they have done well on a research task, there may be more harm in trying to correct this misconception than in permitting it to remain. Conversely, ameliorative efforts are needed when children feel that they have done poorly. In some circumstances, such efforts may include using special experimental procedures to guarantee the child a final experience of success.

Removing Undesirable Consequences of Participating in Research (Principle I)

Most psychological research does no physical damage to participants and minimizes inconvenience to them. The investigator intends no harm, is polite and respectful, informs participants in advance of the duration of the participation, and thanks them for their time and assistance. Human beings, however, can perceive purpose, personal evaluative judgment, and failure in the innocuous or can evince fright during the experiment and shame later.

The instructions and debriefing should include appropriate reassurance to the participants about normal reactions, including disappointment in performance. Investigators familiar with the task and participant population can anticipate most problems. With a change in equipment or sampling population, investigators should include unintentional stressful reactions among the errors to be eliminated. An investigator who does not personally run an experiment remains responsible for training assistants to watch for and correct such stressful reactions and to monitor these as well as other aspects of the experiment. In accordance with Principle C, an instructor supervising graduate or undergraduate research is similarly responsible for teaching students to watch for such stressful reactions and to monitor and correct them.

Sometimes stressful procedures are deliberate and intrinsic to the experiment, as in the research on pain and failure discussed on pages 53–62. The investigator is responsible for correcting observed detrimental effects at the end of the inquiry and for taking reasonable measures to remove those effects that persist after the study is finished.

Whether stressful reactions are accidentally or deliberately produced, investigators should make reasonable efforts to correct those effects that persist after the study is finished.

Principle I. *Where research procedures result in undesirable consequences for the individual participant, the* *investigator has the responsibility to detect and remove or correct these consequences, including long-term effects.*

1. Obligation for Immediately Removing Harmful Effects.

When the participant shows stressful reactions as an immediate consequence of an experimental procedure, it is difficult to justify delay in corrective action. If repeated stressful sessions are necessary, participants should be in a controlled environment between, as well as during, experimental sessions.

Participants should not be dismissed, free to take action that could importantly affect their futures on the basis of such misinformation as, for example, making a decision on whether they should continue to attend classes after being informed that they are not competent to continue in college or pursue a desired career.

2. Long-Term Follow-Up.

Careful debriefing is adequate for most, but not all, participants who have been misinformed or uninformed. In some cases of misinformation or other stressful treatment, a particularly susceptible person may suffer long-term detriment triggered by the experiment. To minimize such risks, investigators may need also to consider participant selection, postexperimental checks, and even long-term follow-ups.

3. Obligations to Vulnerable Populations.

When children, mentally disabled persons, and other vulnerable populations serve as research participants, the investigator assumes a special responsibility to protect their welfare, to give the individuals opportunity to discuss adverse reactions to any part of the research, and to end the session with an appropriate and positive debriefing.

4. Withholding Damaging Information.

At times the investigator may discover things about participants that could be damaging to their self-esteem if revealed. For example, the participant may have performed very poorly at a task and may regard such performance as important. This situation raises the question of whether or not full postinvestigation clarification requires the investigator to disclose such uncomplimentary findings even when they might be only incidental to the main purpose of the research and when the participant does not inquire about them or appear to be aware that information of this nature has been obtained.

In such cases, the investigator becomes involved in a basic conflict of values between the obligation to inform the participant fully, on the one hand, and the desire to avoid harming the participant in any way, on the other. If important damaging information that could affect the subject beyond the experiment (e.g., physical or personality problems) is uncovered, the subject should be informed, although not necessarily by the investigator alone, unless the investigator is qualified to handle the resultant distress (see pages 70–72).

    5. Withholding Potential Benefits From Control Participants.

Some studies involve the use of a drug or of an educational or therapeutic experience hypothesized to have beneficial value for those exposed to it. Typically, the research design requires that this procedure be withheld from persons in a control group.

In connection with Principle G, it has been suggested that the investigator use, as a control comparison, an alternative treatment of known benefit rather than a no-treatment condition. When an alternative treatment is not possible, Principle I implies that the investigator incurs some special responsibility to the control group members because of their participation in the study. Hence, if the new procedures do prove efficacious, efforts should be made at the conclusion of the study to see that the control participants are assured access to them.

The statements above emphasize the investigator's post-research obligations to participants in the deprived control group. There may be corresponding long-term obligations to the participants in the benefited treatment group. For example, patients receiving special therapeutic attention or children receiving nutritional supplements as part of a research procedure may, as a result, develop expectations and dependencies. Termination of the benefits at the end of the research might be damaging to the participants even though the participants seem to be simply left in their initial condition or even benefited by the temporary enrichment involved in the research participation. Investigators, in weighing whether they can ethically undertake the study, must anticipate the development of many expectations or dependencies and assess whether these can be satisfied after the research is terminated.

Anonymity of the Individual and the Confidentiality of Data (Principle J)

The ethical obligations related to maintaining anonymity and confidentiality derive from a widely accepted rule of human conduct. This rule is that every person has, in most aspects of life, a right to privacy that only that person can give permission to violate. Various threats to this right of privacy sometimes occur in research with human beings. For example, the investigator may obtain private information about people without their knowledge. This obtaining of information raises ethical issues related to informed consent treated on pages 34-42 of this report. In addition, having obtained information about research participants with their informed consent, the investigator may later pass it on to others. In so doing, an investigator may violate expectation of confidentiality. Such problems are the subject of discussion in this section.

Clearly, maintaining confidentiality is more important for certain types of information than for others. Religious preferences, sexual practices, income, racial prejudices, and other personal attributes such as intelligence, honesty, and courage are more sensitive items than name, address, and social security number. There are, however, great individual differences in the resistance people would offer to the disclosure of various types of personal information. This consideration argues for a conservative stance, according to which the investigator should be very cautious about revealing any information about research participants.

Another aspect of the problem involves the recipient of the information that is divulged. It is one thing to reveal to a participant's physician evidence of possible drug usage but quite another to provide the local police with the same information. Either disclosure entails serious ethical considerations, but the potential threat to the individual is almost certainly greater in the latter case than in the former. Requests for confidential information may come from many sources—the research participant's relatives and friends, officers of the law, employers, school administrators, the custodians of data banks, even the investigator's professional associates. The demands can be so varied that no simple list can be exhaustive. Again, the investigator must take a position that will protect the research participant from many threats to confidentiality, some of them unexpected.

Finally, some particularly difficult problems arise when the investigator, often by accident, obtains information that perhaps should be disclosed either for the research participant's own protection or for the protection of others. Investigators may learn that research participants use hard drugs, habitually carry a gun, or are on a weight-loss diet that is known to be dangerous. What are the ethical responsibilities of the investigator who discovers such information?

Issues of anonymity, confidentiality, and disclosure of vital personal information are not as clear-cut as they are sometimes thought to be. To the contrary, there are plausible claims from many directions for information the investigator may acquire about research participants. Sometimes the act of protecting their identity and holding facts about them in confidence seems to conflict with the right, rather than simply the desire, of others to know. In extreme cases, maintaining confidentiality may prevent actions needed to protect the welfare—and even the lives—of the participants themselves or of others in contact with them.

Despite these complications, the investigator's primary responsibility is to fulfill the expectation of anonymity and confidentiality with which the research participant enters the research relationship. Principle J reflects this position.

Principle J. **Information obtained about the research participant during the course of an investigation is confidential unless otherwise agreed upon in advance. When the possibility exists that others may obtain access to such information, this possibility, together with plans for protecting confidentiality, is explained to the participant as part of the procedure for obtaining informed consent.**

More often than not, as the principle implies, confidentiality entails a cluster of ethical issues that appear together in a research situation.

1. Maintaining the Participant's Anonymity.

In research where investigators secretly mark the protocols in ways that allow the identification of individuals after promising anonymity, Principle J and also Principle D relating to informed consent are violated. In such research, the investigator has also incurred an obligation to reveal the concealment and deception later on (Principle H), something that may be very difficult to do.

The legitimate needs of research to link different bodies of data concerning the same individuals can be met without violating anonymity. A number of techniques are available to merge data sets while preserving respondent anonymity and should be employed when required.

2. Disclosure to Third Parties.

Typically, the kind of disclosure about which the research participant will be most concerned is whether the information will be made known to particular associates such as parents or friends. Sometimes this objection to disclosure is based on a fear of the damage it might do to the participant's relationships to these close associates; at other times the objection seems to be based more upon the embarrassment to which disclosure might lead. Principle J clearly states that the investigator should not give the requested information to these individuals without the research participant's permission. Maintaining such confidentiality can often be done in a direct and straightforward way, and few problems may be expected to arise.

At other times, however, the situation may be complicated by the fact that associates of the participant (e.g., parents) may feel that they have a right to certain information obtained in the course of research, particularly if they gave the informed consent for participation in the first place. In such cases, there must be an understanding between the investigator and the third party from the beginning as to what information will and will not be made available during or after the experiment. Principle J does not forbid the communication of information to appropriate individuals or groups. In fact, in many cases the transmission of useful data to a teacher or therapist, for example, might greatly benefit the participant. Principle J requires that such data be made available to others only with the free and informed permission of the participant. In the case of data of great importance, however, the investigator may be under an urgent obligation to obtain such consent. This obligation is discussed in Section 6 on deliberate disclosure.

Although problems of confidentiality do not always qualify as ethical problems arising in research, they may arise frequently in situations where personality tests are administered by students to their peers.

3. Disclosure to Organizations of Which the Participant Is a Member.

Investigators are often asked for information about individuals by employers, schools, clinics, or other organizations of which the individual is a member. Since these organizations often initiate the research and support it, their representatives may feel they have a right to the information just as parents sometimes feel they have a right to research data obtained on their children. As discussed in Section 2, Principle J forbids such disclosure without the participant's permission. If no such permission has been obtained, the investigator should keep the data confidential. When research is commissioned or supported by an organization that might later request the data, there should be an explicit agreement regarding the confidentiality of data with participants and the organization in advance.

Maintaining confidentiality may be more difficult for the investigator who is associated with the agency making the request. In such cases, data-collecting procedures that guarantee anonymity are desirable if the research can be done with such methods. If the research cannot be so done, investigators have a first obligation to protect the confidentiality of the data. Failing that, they have a second obligation to inform research participants that their data cannot be kept confidential.

It is possible, of course, to imagine situations in which the investigator is required to collect and transmit sensitive data and the participant is required to provide them, the penalty for not doing so for both parties being loss of employment. Such situations are clearly inimical to the ethical conduct of research.

4. Disclosure to Professional Associates of the Investigator.

The purposes of research often require that data be kept for some time. When the research participants do not have to be recognizable by name, sound ethical practice seems to be to remove identifying data from the research protocol as soon as possible. When the names of individuals must be available, the records may be coded and the key to the code stored where it is accessible to as few people as possible. In the case of very sensitive data, investigators may have to take extreme measures to ensure the inaccessibility of the code.

5. Loss of Confidentiality on the Basis of a Court Order.

The law does not safeguard the confidentiality of all research data. Under a wide range of conditions, an investigator can be legally required to supply information about individuals to the police and the courts, even when the information is collected in the course of research in which confidentiality has been promised to the respondent. The problem becomes particularly pronounced when the information concerns illegal behavior (e.g., use of drugs, violation of sex laws, or participation in illegal demonstrations). Providing information about legal protection is an ethical obligation of psychologists investigating sensitive topics.

The implications of Principle J are as follows: When investigators collect information that has any appreciable likelihood of being demanded by the courts, they should explain the legal situation to the respondent in advance, including the vulnerability of the data, any possible harm its revelation in court might do, and the steps taken to safeguard the information against such revelation. Promising to refuse to honor a court order is promising to break the law, but the investigator can promise to protect the research participant by storing sensitive data in a way that makes the identification of individuals impossible.

6. Deliberate Disclosure to Avoid Greater Harm to the Participant or Harm to Others.

The protection afforded research participants by the maintenance of confidentiality may be compromised when the investigator discovers information that serious harm threatens the research participant or others. The obligation to make this information known to research participants, their associates, or legal authorities nonetheless creates an ethical dilemma in consideration of the promised maintenance of strict confidentiality. The obligation to disclose such information derives from more general ethical principles than those that are strictly limited to scientific research. Principle J, however, places a special obligation on investigators to inform the individual that the information may have to be disclosed. The research participant should be carefully counseled about the limits of confidentiality and, in this particular case, the justification for transmitting information to someone else. Investigators also should realize that they may very well have incurred a responsibility for long-term follow-up attention to the disturbed individual as is described in pages 66–67 of this report.

A body of case law governing the behavior of the investigator with respect to disturbed participants may accumulate, as has already occurred regarding client-therapist relationships.

   7. Loss of Confidentiality Through Research Publications.

When aggregate data are published, loss of confidentiality is seldom a problem. However, when the mode of communicating the results involves presentation of case material on well-known individuals or aggregate data on a narrow population or an identified or deducible organization (e.g., a small village or a corporation), specific individuals may be recognized and sensitive information about them revealed, either to professionals familiar with the research setting or to others who may read the report. In many cases, of course, the data revealed do not constitute a threat to anyone's well-being. In studies of human sensory functioning, it is actually a custom to report data by the observer's initials, a practice that very often identifies the individual. Principle J permits this practice, given informed consent by the person thus identified.

The same reasoning applies to more difficult cases. When the mode of publication involves detailed presentation of sensitive data on individuals who are likely to be known to some readers, so that identifying individuals and learning sensitive information about them are possible, then the extent of this risk should be made known to such persons and their consent to the mode of publication obtained, both at the outset of the research and after they have seen the specific report. Attempts should be made to disguise the individuals and disassociate sensitive material from them to the extent that such can be done without jeopardizing the research.

   8. Loss of Confidentiality Through Data Banks.

Data banks develop as research needs require the collation of diverse information about individuals, permitting important analyses that would not otherwise be possible. Problems arise when confidential, private, or potentially damaging information about persons are included in the bank or when cumulative data on individuals invade their privacy, although no single piece of information is particularly sensitive. If the information in a data bank identifies the individual, it may be used to that individual's disadvantage. The data bank may be managed in a way that does not safeguard confidentiality. The investigator may not wish to contribute data to a data bank because people who will have access to the data are not adequately trained or motivated to interpret them accurately. The investigator may be reluctant to contribute to the data bank without having obtained informed consent to do so. Principle J clarifies the investigator's obligation in the situation. Research participants should be informed of the immediately proposed use of the data, and their consent for such use must be obtained. In addition, it is recommended that participants be informed that anonymous data may be released for re-analysis and that consent be obtained for this eventuality.

Even with the consent of research participants, the investigator should ask the following questions: Are there adequate safeguards to protect the confidentiality of the information? Are the data sensitive? Could participants reasonably object to the potential use of the data? Could the data be used, even indirectly, to the disadvantage of the individuals involved? Unless appropriate answers to these questions are forthcoming, the data should not be released to the data bank.

9. Confidentiality of Information About the Participant's Valued Groups.

Sometimes a problem of confidentiality involves the individual participant's valued groups. The concept of betraying confidentiality "by category" arises when research reveals things that may be seen as degrading these groups.

This issue presents the investigator with a severe value conflict. On one side is an obligation to research participants who may not wish to see derogatory information (in whose validity they will probably not believe) published about their valued groups. On the other side is an obligation to publish findings one believes relevant to scientific progress, an objective that in the investigator's view will contribute to the eventual understanding and amelioration of social and personal problems.

Such value conflicts can sometimes be resolved before a problem arises. When the problem may be anticipated before the data are collected, the investigator will be wise to include information about potential uses of the data in the explanation provided to the potential research participants at the time of their recruitment to the study. The participants may then give informed and uncoerced consent to participate, knowing in advance that there may be unpalatable items among the research outcomes. The issue, in fact, is conceived better perhaps as one of informed consent not as one of confidentiality.

To make this suggestion is not to diminish the magnitude of the dilemma under consideration. The investigator must be constantly aware that many potential topics of study are emotionally and politically explosive. Just as investigators are sensitive to their scientific responsibilities, they must also be sensitive to the social, political, and human implications of the interpretations that others might place upon this research once the findings have been published.

INDEX

Page numbers appearing in *italics* indicate pages on which an ethical principle is actually stated or on which primary discussion of a principle appears.

A

Aged, research with, 16, 56
Agreement, explicitness of, 5, 30, 31, *32*
Agreement, fairness of, 5, 30, 31
Agreement, fulfillment of, 5, 31, 33
Alcohol, use in research, 57
Alternative procedures, 54, 59
Alternatives to research participation, 47, 52
Angering participants, avoiding, 63, 64
Animals, research with, 52, 54
Anonymity, 7, 37, 39, 58, 68, 70-71
Anonymous naturalistic observation, *37*
Assistants, responsibility of, 5, 21, 27, 30, 66

B

Benefit
 of research, 19, 20, 21, 22, 23, 27, 47, 48
 of treatment, 18, 20, 22, 32, 56, 61
Biased data, 18, 19
Biased judgments, 20

C

Certification, 50
Clients of nonmandatory service organizations, *46*
Children, research with, 22, 31, 33-34, 55, 56, 59, 63, 65-66, 68, 71
Clinical settings, research in, 21, 46
Coercion, 32-33, 42-51
Collaborative research, 27, 30
Collegial review, 20, 21; *see also* consultation with others.
Commitments, honoring, 31, 33, 64
Competence to give informed consent, 33-34
Concealment, 6, 17, 34-42
Confidentiality, 7, 18, 37, 39, 40, 58, 68, 70, 72-74
 loss through court order, 72
 loss through data banks, 73-74
 loss through publication, 73
Consultation with others, 5, 20-21, 26, 27-29, 34, 36, 40, 41, 45, 46; *see also* collegial review
Control participants, 17, 18, 54, 68
Co-principle investigators, 27, 30
Cost/benefit analysis, 27, 29
Cross-cultural research, 21, 22
Covert observation, 28, 36, 37-38

D

Data banks, 69, *73*
Debriefing, 41, 61, 65
Deception, 6, 17, 19, 34-42, 47, 60
Deception to obtain agreement to participate, *41*
Disclosure of information, to avoid harm to participant, *70*, 72
Discontinuation of participation, *50, 56-57*
Disguised field experimentation, 36, *38*
Disillusioning participants, avoiding, 63, 64
"Double deception", 65
Drugs, use of in research, 28, 54, 56, *57-58*, 68, 69

E

Economic and social background differences, 20
Educational research, 45, 47, 68
Electric shock, 51, 53, 55, 61
Employees, research with, 21, 31
Ethnic group differences, research on, 20, 28
Exploitation of the participant, 30, 31, 53

F

Federal regulations, 43, 54, 58
Financial support, source of, 22-24

G

Guardian, informed consent of, 33-34

H

Handicapped persons, research with, 16
Harmful procedures, 17, 18, 26, 47, *51-62*
Hospitals, research in, 21, 22, 45
Human rights, 16

I

Incredulity regarding debriefing, *65*
Inducements to motivate participation, 43, 48
Industrial research, 49-50
Industrial settings, recruiting participants in, 22, 49-50
Informed consent, 17, 18, 22, 26, 29, 32, 33, 35, 36, 38, 40, 45, 51, 53, 56, *57*, 60, 73, 74
Inmates of mandatory institutions, research with, *44*; *see also* institutional settings
Institutional Review Boards, 20, 25, 29, 34, 47
Institutional settings, research in, 44, 56
Invasion of privacy, 17, 27, 37, 39, 68, 73
Involvement of persons in research without their knowledge or consent, 38-40
Irreversible aftereffects, 62

J

Judgment, contexts that may affect, 25

L

Lack of interest of the subject, 65
Licensure, 50
Long-term effects and follow-up, 7, *67, 72*

M

Medical consultation, 29
Mentally disabled, research with, 16, 31, 33-34, 44, 56, 67; *see also* vulnerable groups
Methodological requirements, 6, 34-35
Military research, 39, *50*
Military settings, recruiting participants in, 21, 22, 50
Misconceptions, 6, 62-66
Misinformation, 34, 40, 62
Misleading results, 18, 19
Misuse of data, 23
Multiple-session research, *64-65*

N

Naturally occurring conditions, 59
Negative aftereffects, 37

O

Observational research, 37
Old, 16; *see also* aged

P

Participant-observation research, *38*
Payment for participation, 33, 43
Phenominological investigations, 59
Physical stress, protection from, 6, *53-58*
Pilot studies, 26
Poor, research with, 16
Post-experimental information, 41, 61, 65, 67
Principle A, *5*, 25-30, *26*, 36
Principle B, *5*, 25-30, *26*, 34
Principle C, *5*, 25-30, 27, 66
Principle D, *5,* 30-34, *31*, 34, 36, 40, 41, 53, 60, 70
Principle E, 6, 32, 34-42, *35*
Principle F, *6*, 31, 32, 34, 35, 41, *42*, 42-52, 53
Principle G, *6,* 51-62, *53,* 68
Principle H, *6,* 35, 41, 62-65, 59, 62-66, *63,* 70
Principle I, *7,* 41, 45, 53, 59, 60, 62, *66,* 66-68
Principle J, *7,* 40, 58, 68-74, *70*
Prisoners, research with, 43, 44, 45, 49
Prisons, research in, 21, 31, 49
Proprietary rights over research results, 23
Psychological stress, 58-62

Public behavior, recording of, 36-38
Publication of research findings, 23, 75
Punishment, 48

R

Recruiting practices, 48, 51, 57
Refusal to participate, 18, *50*
Regulatory considerations, 19, 22, 33, 54, 58
Removal of harmful effects, 21, 41, 53, 66-68
Responsibility of investigator, 5, 20, 21, 27, 29-30, 35, 53, 66, 71, 74
Restricting access to research data, 23
Risk, 6, 18, 20, 21, 22, 25, 26, 27, 28, 29, 31, 37, 38, 44, 49, 67
Role-playing studies, 59

S

Safety precautions, 55
Screening of participants, 55*,* 67
Service contexts, research in, 21, 22
Service provider, research with, 49-50
Sex, differences in, 20, 28
Sponsorship of research, 23, 49
Spread of risk, 44, 50
Stressful procedures, exposure to, 6, 17, 18, 28, 51, 58
Students, research with, 32-33, 47-48, 64
Subject pool, 32, 42, 47-48
Supervisor, responsibility of, 30
Surrogate consent, 33-34

T

Third parties
 obtaining information from, 36, *40*
 disclosure to, *70*

U

Undesirable consequences, removal of, 7, *66-68*
Unobtrusive measures, 37
Utilization of research results, 23

V

Vulnerable groups, research with, 16, 31, 47, 56, 67; *see also* aged, children, mentally disabled, prisoners

W

Withdrawal of data, 41, *42,* 51
Withdrawal of participation, 6, 18, 33, 34, 41, 47, 48, 50
Withholding damaging information, 67
Withholding treatment or benefits, 17, 54, *68*

BF
200
.A46
1982x
c.2

A.P.A.

American Psychological
   Association. Committee
   for the Protection of
   Human Participants in
   Research.
      Ethical principles in the
   conduct of research with human
      participants